Red Leaves & Golden Curtains

Photographs by Maxine Henryson
Essay by Mario Kramer

For my father and mother,
Melville and Louise

Red Leaves & Golden Curtains

In *Red Leaves & Golden Curtains,* I explore my perception of the feminine in the world, examining the differences and similarities between cultures. The project traces evidence of divinity, rituals, place, memory, and history in the West and the East.

Taken in the United States, France, Germany, Belgium, Italy, Poland, Russia, India, and Cambodia, the photographs represent intimate moments when external reality mirrors my internal reality. Using the immediacy of the visual diary to invoke specific but often inexplicable emotions, I create abstract, painterly photographs. Figuration is balanced with abstraction, physicality with ephemerality, and an investigation of light and film with autobiographical references.

I observe how natural phenomena are recorded by the camera. Photographing the atmospheres and color tonalities of contrasting cultural landscapes, I experiment through the lens creating a complex conjunction between personal (subjective) reality and transpersonal (observed) reality.
Memory and time collide.

Maxine Henryson

The Visible Time

"To collect photographs is to collect the world."
Susan Sontag, On Photography, N.Y. 1979

Since the early 1990s, Maxine Henryson has created pictures of her internal landscape using color photography. The result is a painterly style which transcends the literal and realistic. The New York based artist has traveled extensively for her work to Europe, Russia, and repeatedly to Asia. Shimmering red autumn leaves in Vermont, a stairway in the Palazzo Rezzonico in Venice, or the entrance area of the Ekambareswara Temple in Kanchipuram – the images are transformed by Henryson into a flow of light and color. What emerges is simultaneously lyrical and dynamic.

Landscapes, interiors, street scenery, still life, even static architecture is lent a sense of motion. Space and time are extended, compositional elements and figures blur until they appear to form a new reality. Despite the ever-changing themes of mood, light, and culture, Maxine Henryson's work is highly coherent and conceptual. The vocabulary of these very precisely composed images is reduced and focused on the essential – nothing is added. These color photographs impress us with their enormous variety of nuance as well as a calm contemplative expressiveness.

Movement is at the core of many of Maxine Henryson's images and often alters our perception of the subject. She achieves this by handholding long exposures with a Leica rangefinder and intentionally playing with the focus of a single lens reflex camera. She likes to describe this approach as a "calculated coincidence." The floating world of Henryson's photographic images is a quiet one, the images seeming secretive as they narrate a story about both presence and absence. The suites of photographs present their individual moods of composition and color. Thus, the sequences from St. Petersburg, Germany, or Poland have a rather intense, almost melancholic tone, in comparison to the luminous color found in the photographs from South India or Cambodia. The photographs are connected to one another as though they are ghostly travel memories evoking the sense of having a vague and condensed reminiscence of past journeys and distant places, all centered on the idea of light. Maxine Henryson feels bound to street photography in the tradition of Helen Levitt. Photographing spontaneously, she has an instinctive perception of the fleeting moment.

Another important constant in Henryson's work is her study of time and timelessness. There are very few visual icons in her work, like cars or advertising, to indicate when the photographs were taken. Her images seem to reflect fragments from our collective unconscious.

In the works of Maxine Henryson we visit sacred places such as the Pardesi Synagogue, Kochi, the Mother of God in San Giovanni Crisostomo, Venice, or an altar in the Sera Je Buddhist Monastery, Bylakuppe. These images are a celebration of the complexity of human existence. With her photographs, Maxine Henryson succeeds in relating to us the coexistence of seemingly disparate ideas like materialism and spirituality or nature and culture.

Through a refined and studied use of blurriness, her objective is not to make the subject disappear but to evoke it by means of light. Thereby the unfocused subject forms a resonant space with a high degree of abstraction, which reflects distance and proximity at the same time. The work lets us pause for a moment and demands a detailed survey. The photographs pull the viewer into the depth of the picture ground. Especially in her more recent large-scale photographs, Henryson succeeds in focusing the viewer on her images and her seductive use of light. The feelings below the surface, the layers beneath the visible, allow us to experience our own emotions as though reflected in a mirror. Not surprisingly, mirrors and windows are recurring themes in Henryson's work. The often-observed motifs of curtains or draperies reveal more than they hide. Henryson's journey also winds through the four seasons, paying witness to snowfall, blooming fruit trees, cool marble church walls, the burning heat of ritual temple fires, summer fruits, and the autumn foliage of a Vermont Indian summer.

The pictures seem to glow before us as we see the changes in light during the passage of the day. Their intimacy moves us while it elicits a sense of the sublime. In this sense the photographs of Maxine Henryson are pictures of both memories and wishes. These photographs are the new painting.

Mario Kramer
Curator of the Collection
Museum für Moderne Kunst
Frankfurt am Main, Germany

Die belichtete Zeit

„To collect photographs is to collect the world."
Susan Sontag, On Photography, N.Y. 1979

Seit den frühen 1990er Jahren schafft Maxine Henryson mit ihren Farbfotografien Bilder einer inneren Landschaft. Impressionistischen Gemälden vergleichbar erzeugen sie beim Betrachter eine Wahrnehmung, die weit über den abgebildeten Gegenstand hinausreicht. Ausgedehnte Reisen in den vergangenen Jahren haben die in New York lebende Künstlerin nach Europa, Russland und immer wieder nach Asien geführt. Ob rotleuchtendes Herbstlaub in Vermont, ein Treppenhaus im Palazzo Rezzonico in Venedig oder der Eingangsbereich des Ekambareswara-Tempels in Kanchipuram, die Motive werden in einen Strom aus Licht und Farbe umgesetzt. Die dabei entstandenen Aufnahmen sind lyrisch bewegte Fotografien.

Landschaften, Interieurs, Straßenszenen, Stillleben, selbst statische Architekturen geraten in Bewegung. Raum und Zeit werden gedehnt, Bildelemente und Konturen verschmelzen zu malerischen Eindrücken und modellieren eine neue Einheit. Alles scheint mit allem in Verbindung zu stehen durch ein Fließen von Licht und Farbe. Trotz der unterschiedlichen Sujets dieser Fotografien ist das Werk Maxine Henrysons konzeptuell und stilistisch ausgesprochen kohärent. Das Bildvokabular dieser sehr präzise komponierten Bilder ist reduziert und auf das Wesentliche konzentriert, nichts ist inszeniert. Die ausschließlich in Farbe aufgenommenen Fotografien beeindrucken durch einen enormen Reichtum an Nuancen und eine ruhige, kontemplative Ausstrahlung.

Die Motive werden mit Bewegung ins Bild gesetzt, wobei Maxine Henryson für die Fotografien längere Belichtungszeiten wählt und die Kamera selbst im Moment der Aufnahme bewegt. Dafür nutzt sie die Möglichkeiten einer leicht handhabbaren 35 mm Leica mit einem Entfernungsmesser und spielt intentional mit dem Fokus einer Single-Lens-Reflex-Camera. Man kann diese Vorgehensweise auch als den kalkulierten Zufall beschreiben. Maxine Henryson ist dabei auf der Suche nach langsamen und stillen Bildern. Henrysons fotografische Bildwelt gleicht einer Art Schwebezustand. Die Aufnahmen bewahren jedoch ein Geheimnis, indem sie von Gegenwart und Abwesenheit zugleich erzählen. Die Werkgruppen haben jeweils einen ganz eigenen Stimmungswert und Farbklang. So haben die Sequenzen aus St. Petersburg, Deutschland oder Polen einen eher tiefen, melancholischen Ton im Vergleich zur fast glühenden Farbigkeit der Motive aus Südindien oder Kambodscha. Übrig bleibt schemenhaft verdichtet die fixierte Erinnerung an das, was wir von einer solchen Reise, solch fernen Orten zu wissen glauben: die Idee des Lichts. Maxine Henryson sieht sich einer Street Photography in der Tradition von Helen Levitt verpflichtet. Ein instinktives Wahrnehmen des Augenblicks. Es entsteht nicht eine Bilderflut, sondern eher das Einzelbild.

Eine weitere bedeutende Konstante im Werk von Henryson bildet ihre Auseinandersetzung mit der Komplexität von Zeit. Selten gibt ein Fahrzeug oder städtische Architektur, zum Beispiel Leuchtreklame, darüber Auskunft, in welcher Zeit die Aufnahmen entstanden sind. Gerade diese Zeitlosigkeit ist eine Qualität dieser Bilder. Zeit- und fast körperlos scheinen sie dem kollektiven Gedächtnis entnommen. Man könnte auch von einer imaginativen Vision der Fotografin sprechen.

Wir begegnen im Werk von Maxine Henryson immer wieder mystischen Orten wie der Synagoge der jüdischen Gemeinde von Cochin in Kerala, dem Gnadenbild der Muttergottes in S. Giovanni Crisostomo in Venedig oder einem buddhistischen Altarraum in Bylakuppe. Diese Bilder feiern die Spiritualität der menschlichen Existenz. Maxine Henryson stößt mit ihren Fotografien in die Sphäre der Transzendenz vor. Es gelingt ihr eine Koexistenz von Materialität und Spiritualität, von Natur- und Kulturkosmos.

Bei dem gezielten Einsatz der Unschärfe geht es nicht um das Verschwinden des Gegenstandes, sondern vielmehr um seine Evokation mittels Licht. Die Unschärfe bildet dabei einen Klangraum mit hohem Abstraktionsgrad, der zugleich Distanz und Nähe widerspiegelt. Das Werk lässt einen innehalten und fordert Zeit zum genauen Betrachten. Die Bilder haben eine Sogwirkung in die Tiefe des Bildgrundes. Gerade durch die neueren Großformate gelingt es Henryson, den Betrachter noch stärker auf ihre Bilder und den Sog ihres Lichts zu konzentrieren. Die unter der Bildoberfläche liegenden Gefühle, die Ebenen hinter dem Sichtbaren, erlauben uns wie in einem Spiegel auch unsere eigenen Emotionen wahrzunehmen. Spiegel und Fenster sind daher immer wiederkehrende Motive im Werk von Henryson. Die ebenfalls häufigen Motive der Vorhänge oder Trapperien zeigen mehr, als sie verhüllen. Schneefall und blühende Obstbäume, kühler Marmor von Kirchenwänden und glühende Hitze von rituellen Tempelfeuern, die Früchte des Sommers und das Herbstlaub des Indien Summers in Vermont begleiten uns wie die vier Jahreszeiten auf der Reise durch dieses Buch.

Die Bilder leuchten regelrecht im differenzierten Licht der unterschiedlichen Tageszeiten in unsere Gegenwart hinüber. Ihre Intimität berührt uns. Der Zyklus dieser Aufnahmen ruft ein Gefühl des Sublimen hervor. Die Fotografien von Maxine Henryson sind in diesem Sinne Erinnerungs- und Wunschbilder zugleich. Es handelt sich um Malerei mittels der Fotografie.

Mario Kramer
Kustos der Sammlung
Museum für Moderne Kunst
Frankfurt am Main

Biography

Maxine Henryson is a color photographer who creates poetically and spiritually motivated projects. Born in Jackson, Mississippi and raised in Hopedale, Massachusetts, she received a B.S. from Simmons College in sociology. She completed her M.Phil. at the University of London in sociology, M.A.T. at the University of Chicago in studio arts, and M.F.A. at the University of Illinois at Chicago in photography. Her photographs have been widely exhibited in the United States and Europe and are in numerous collections including the Celanese Photography Collection Frankfurt am Main, the Russian Museum, St. Petersburg, and the Norton Museum of Art, West Palm Beach.

In April of 2003, her artist book, *Presence,* was released. The expressionistic color photographs have been called by Mario Kramer, curator of the Museum für Moderne Kunst Frankfurt am Main, Germany, "the new painting." Her photographs have appeared in the *New Yorker, The New York Times, New York Magazine,* and *NÅMARÌPA Categories of Indian Thought* as well as in many other publications. Maxine Henryson has taught photography at the University of Chicago Laboratory Schools, International Center of Photography, City University of New York, and Bennington College. For the past seven years Henryson has been studying ashtanga yoga as taught by guru Sri K. Pattabhi Jois of Mysore, India. She peripatetically enters and exits the cultural landscapes where she lives and works – New York City, Vermont, Europe, and South Asia.

Red Leaves & Golden Curtains

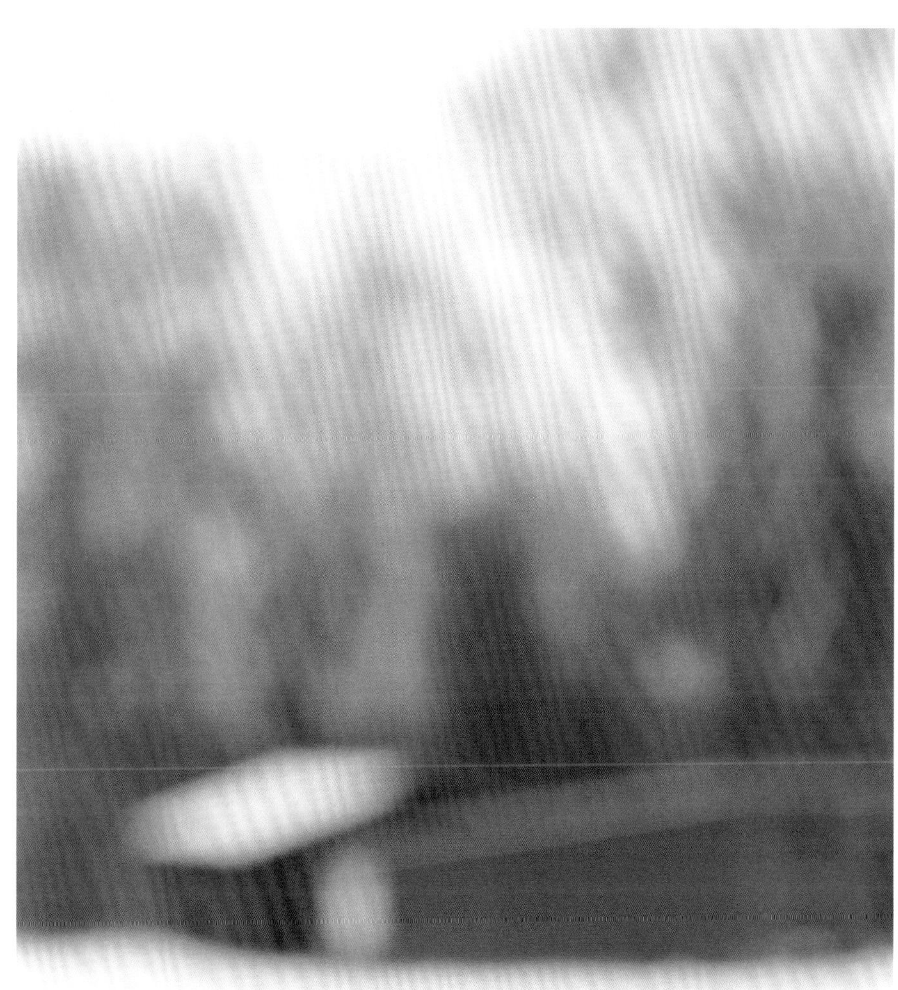

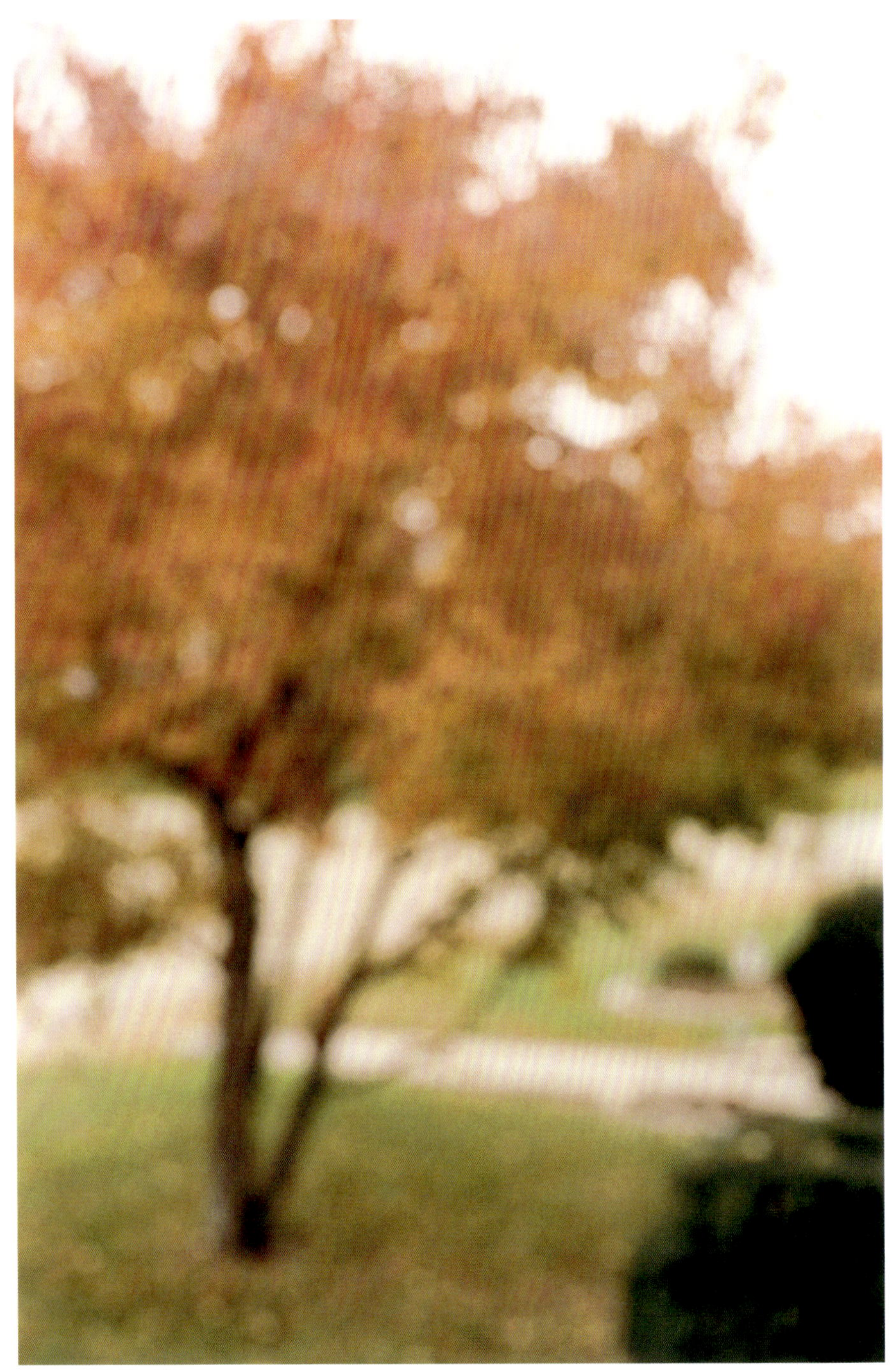

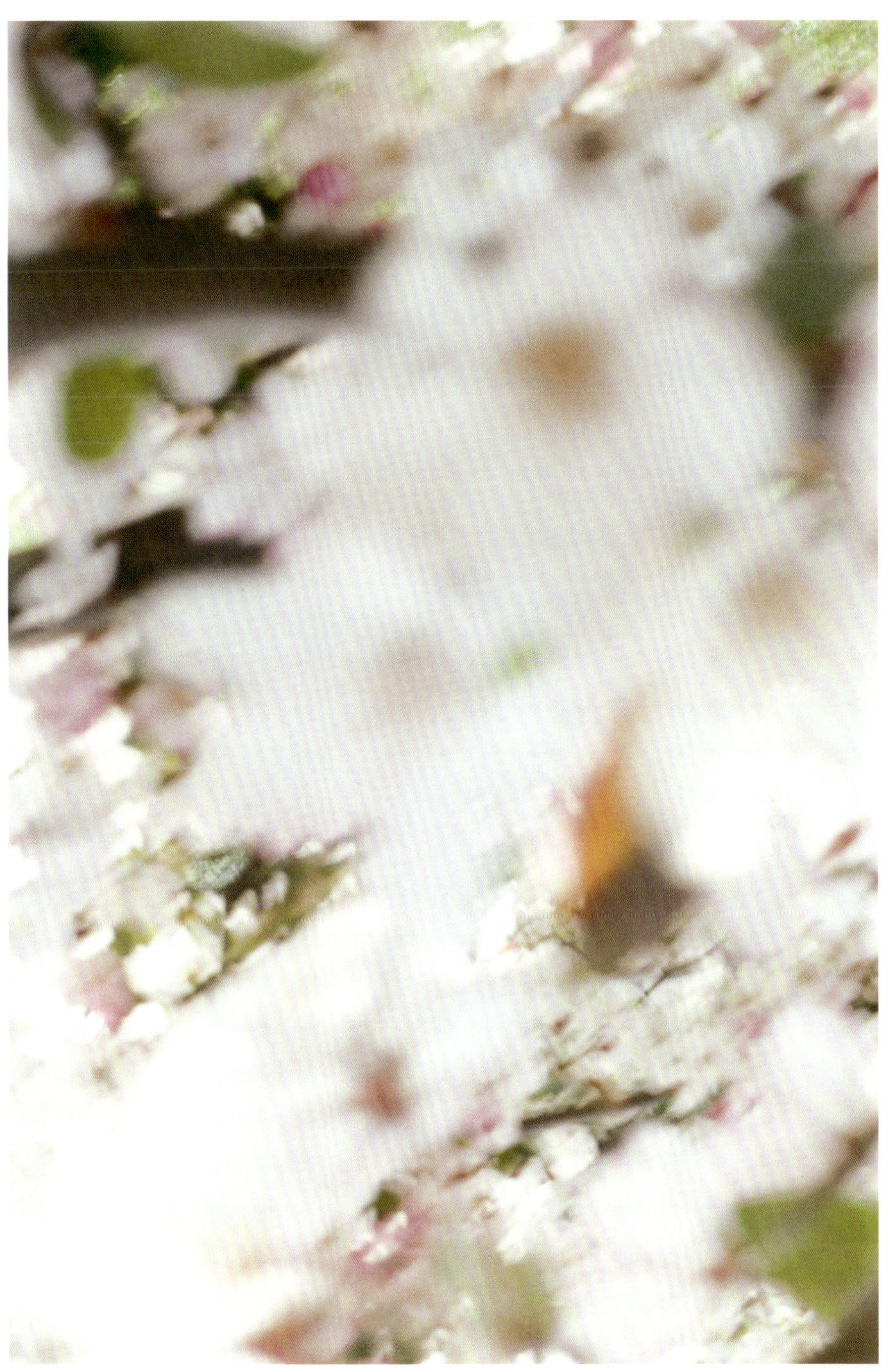

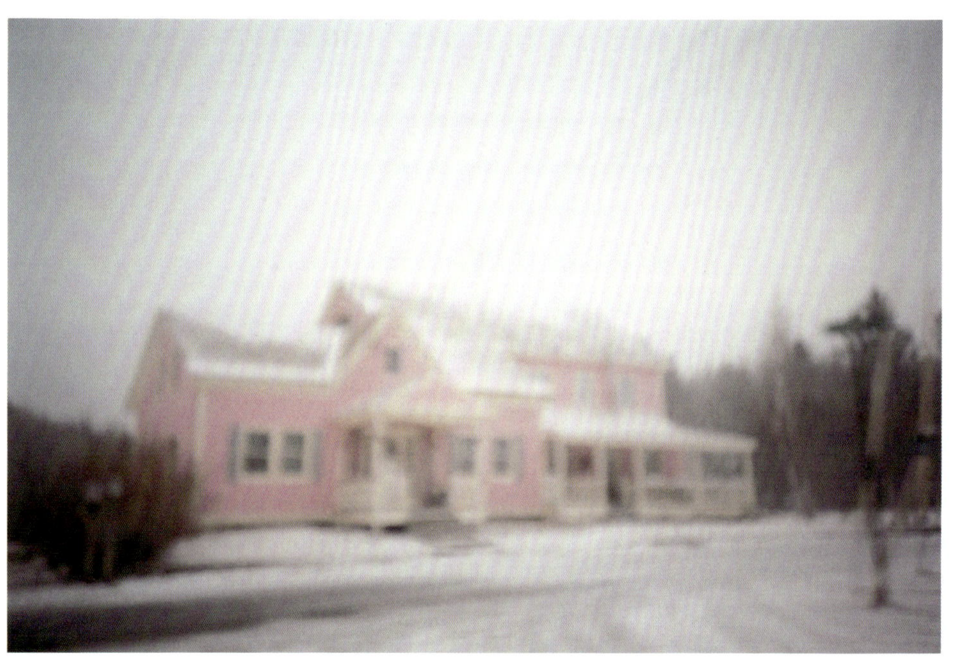

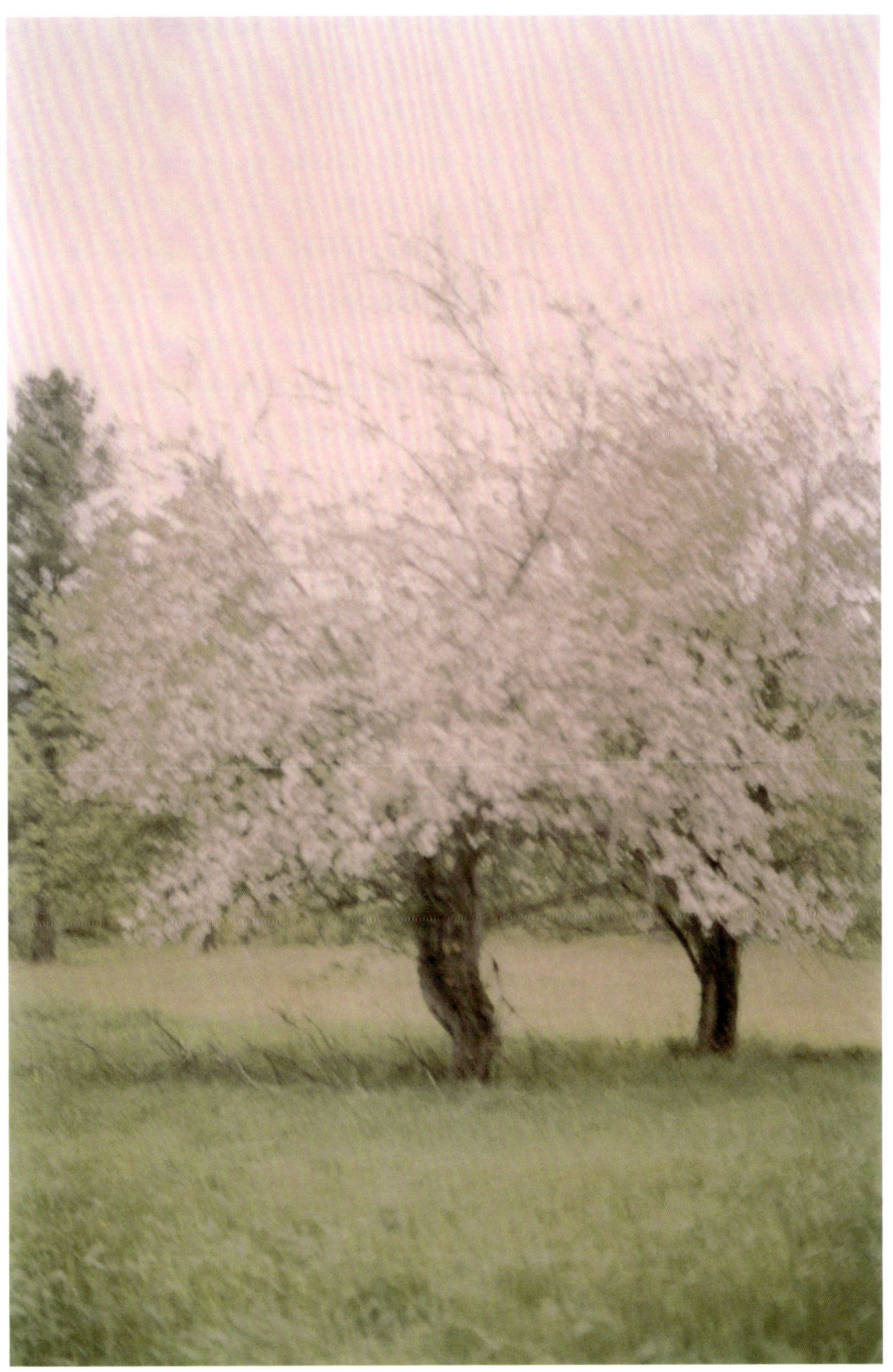

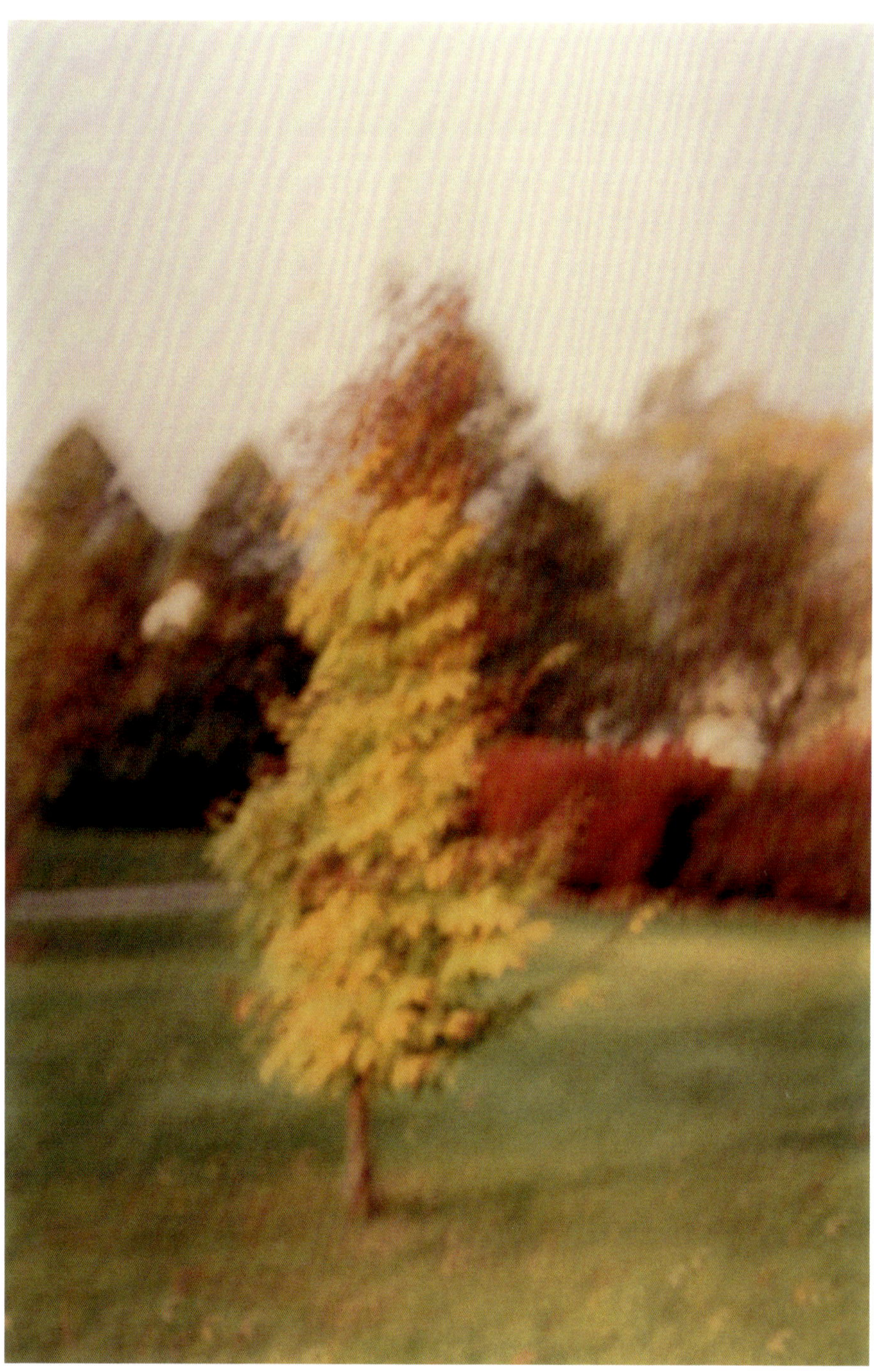

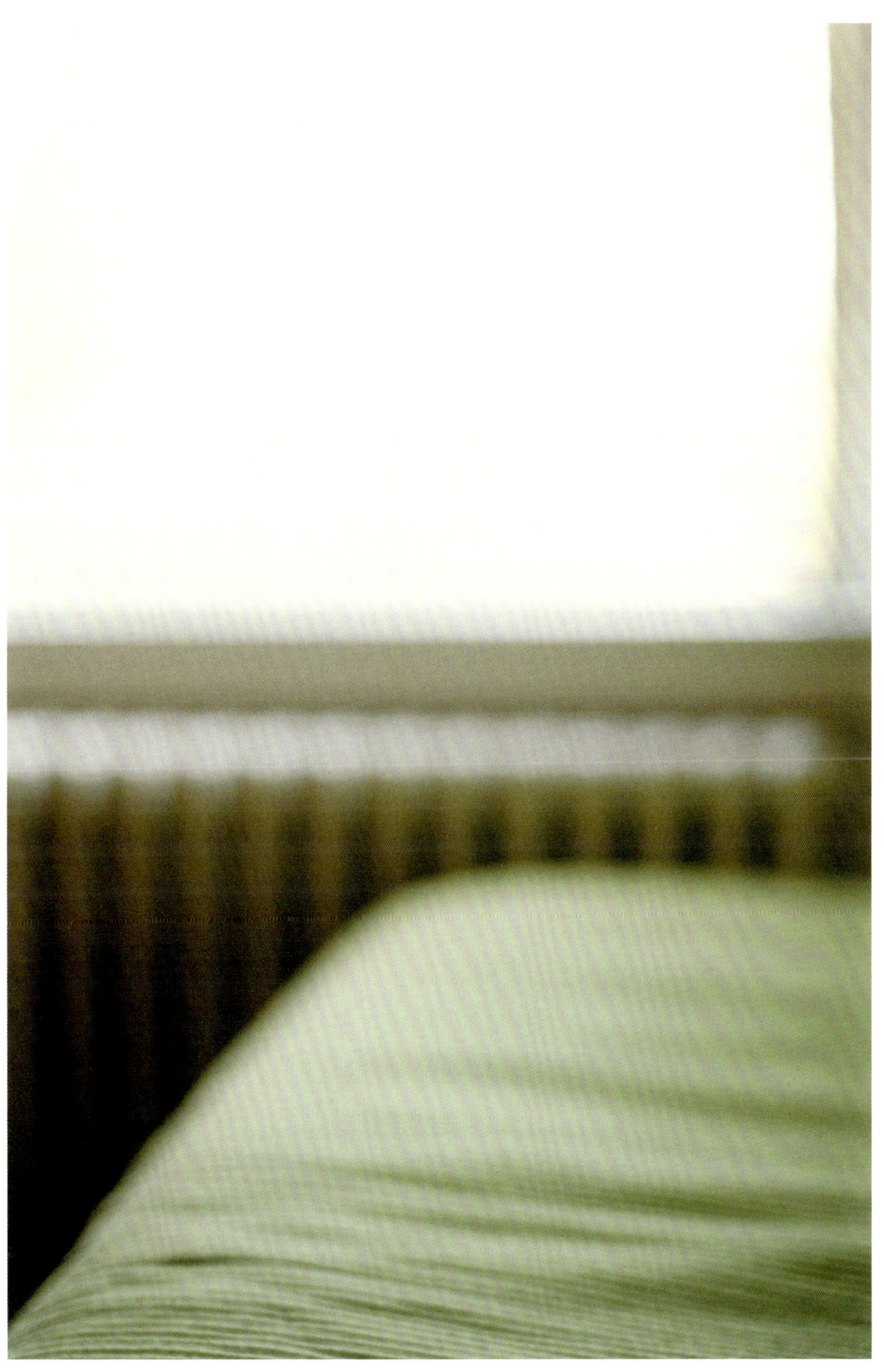

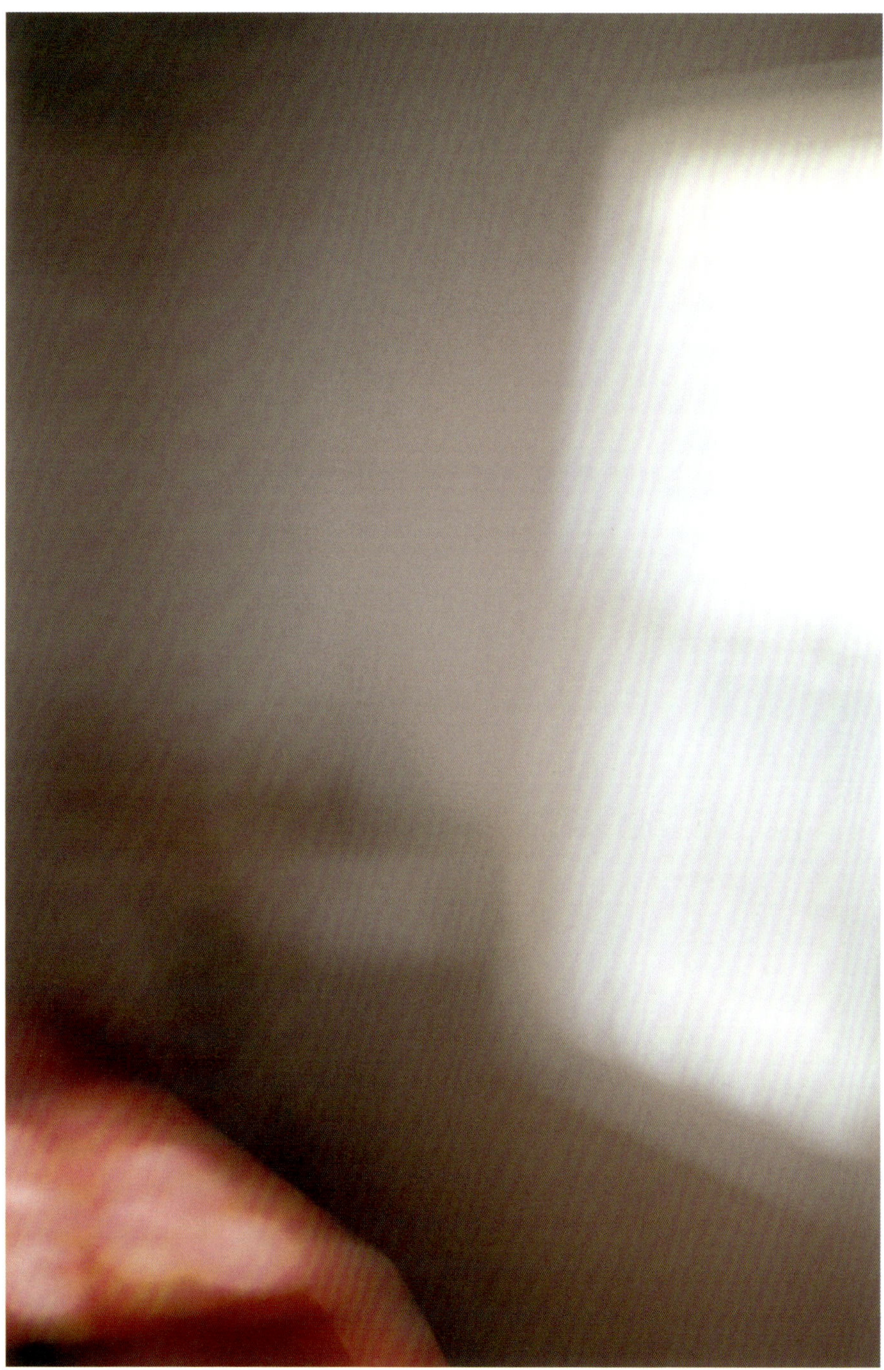

9

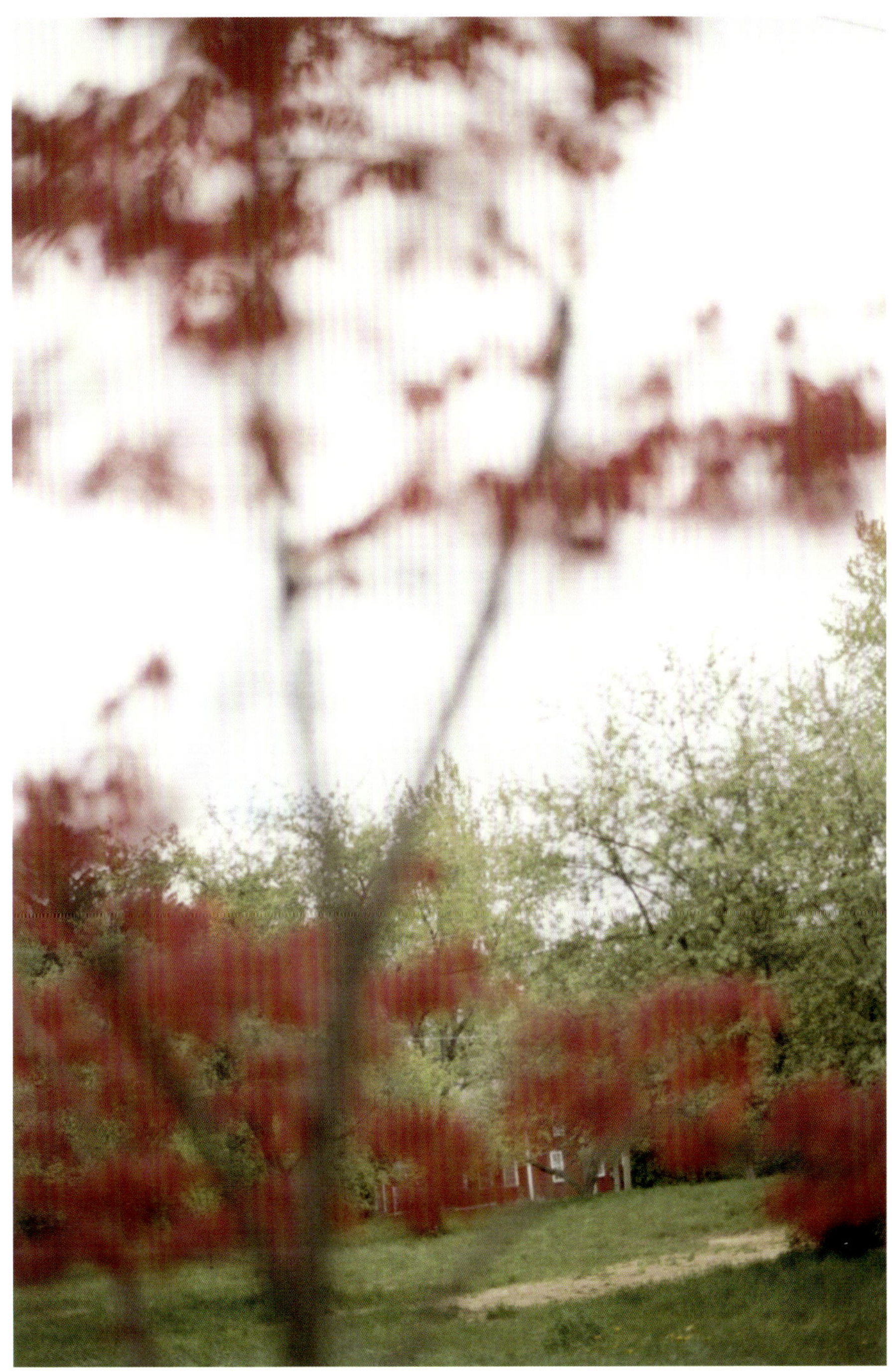

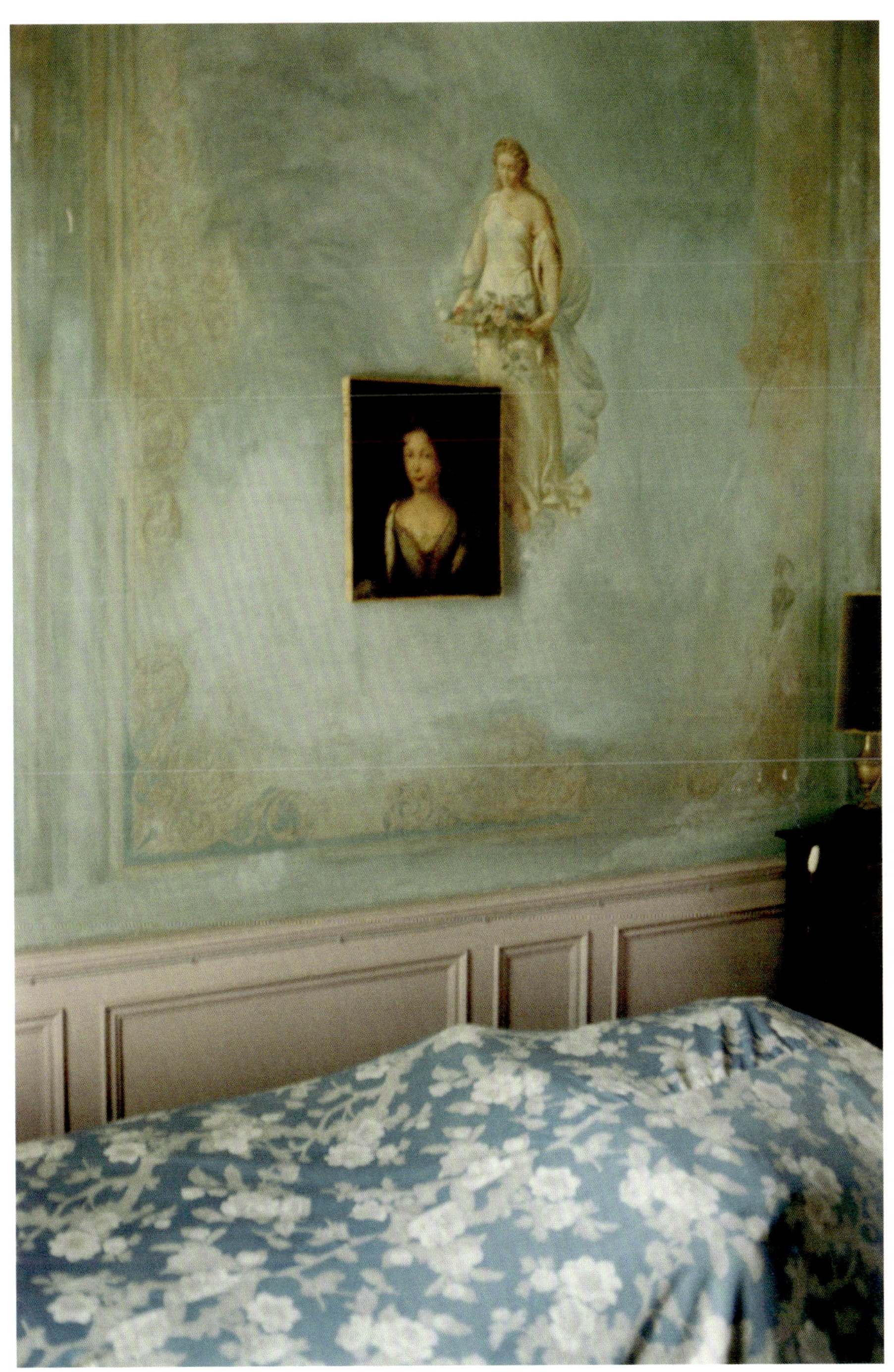

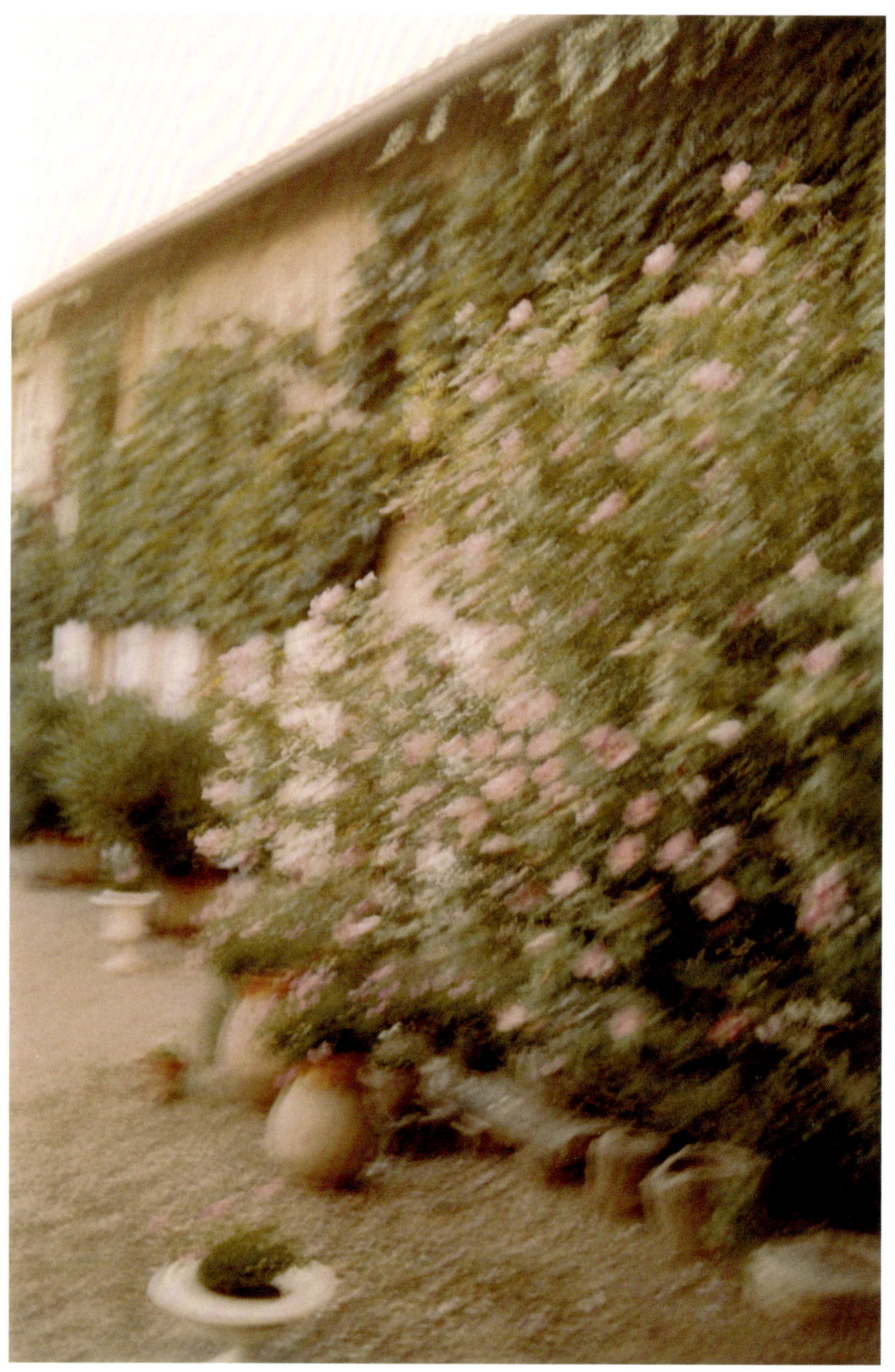

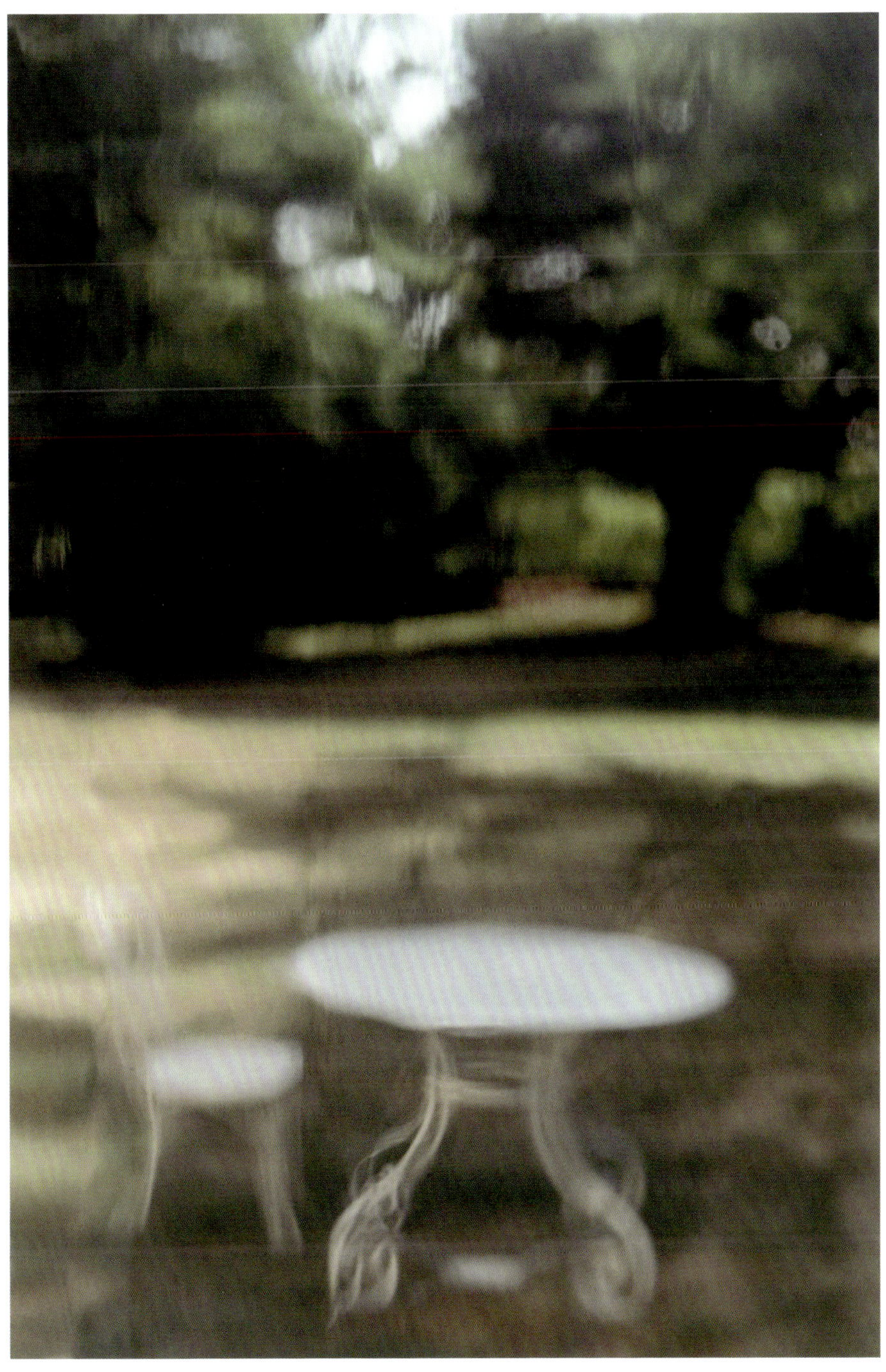

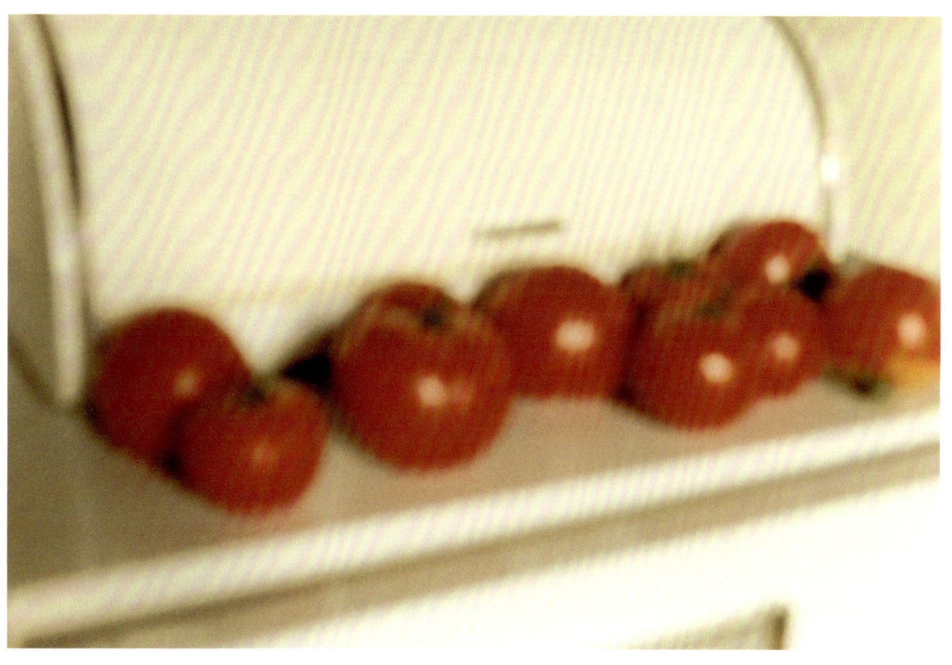

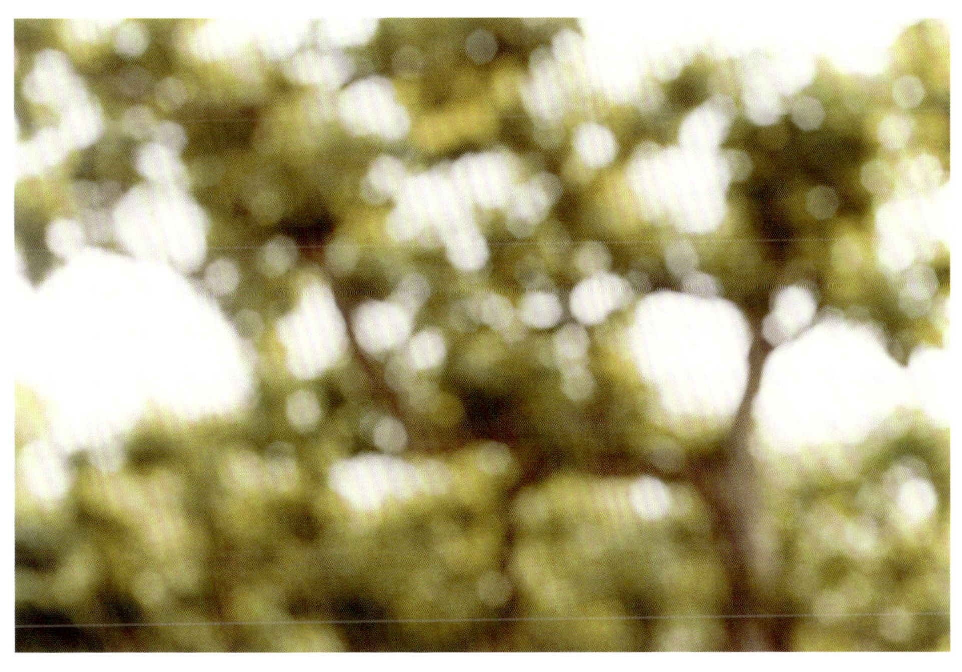

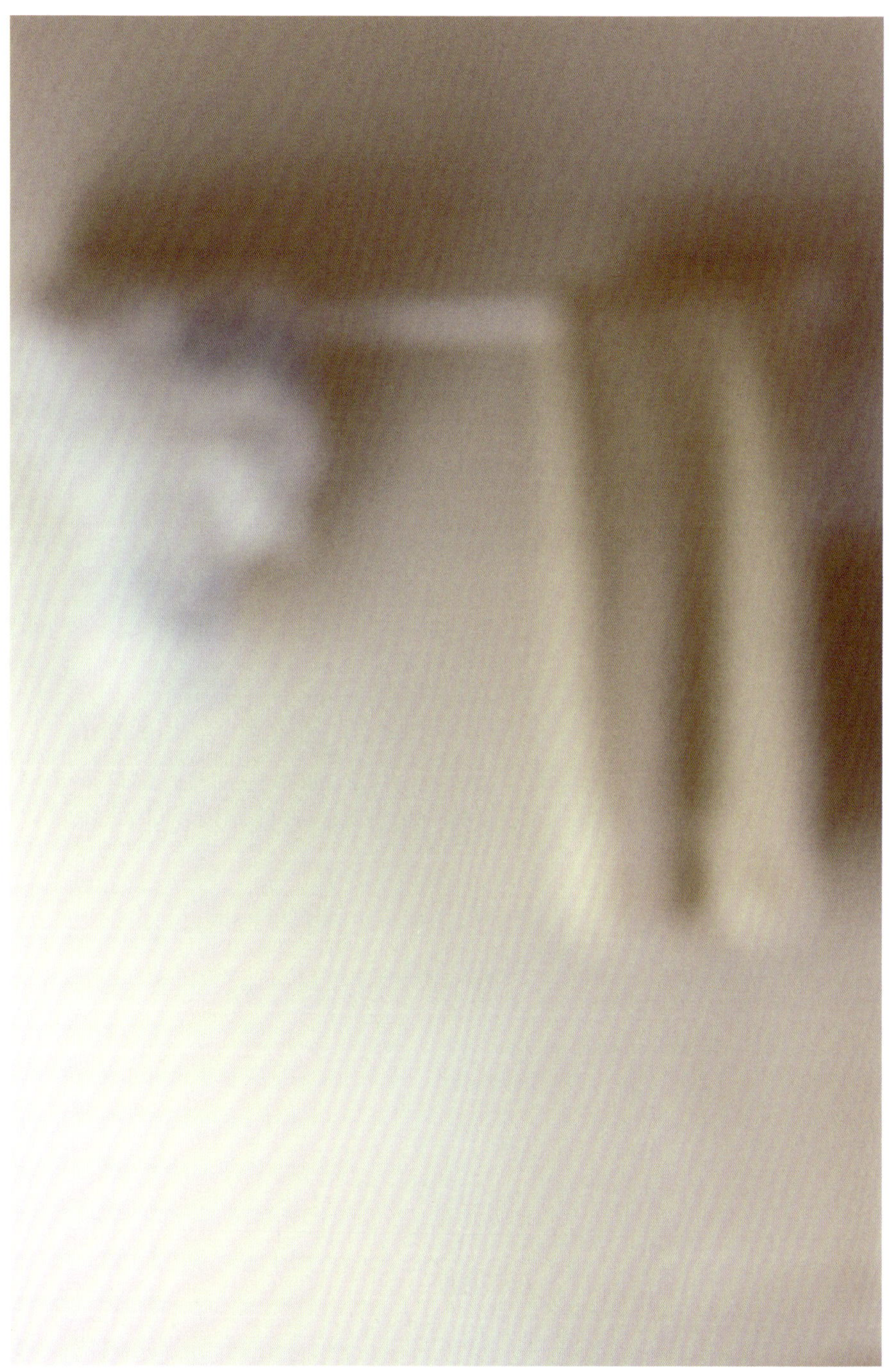

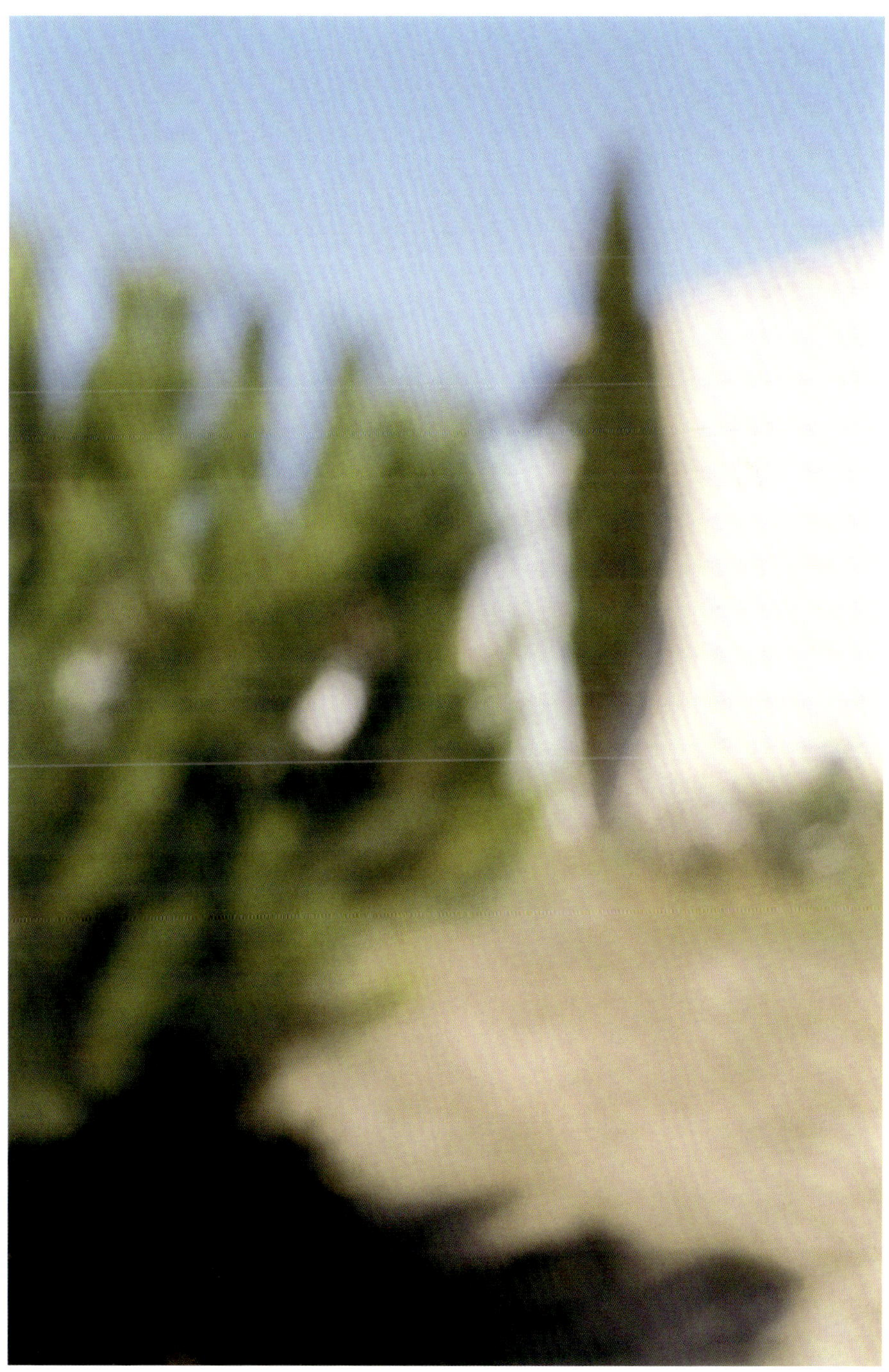

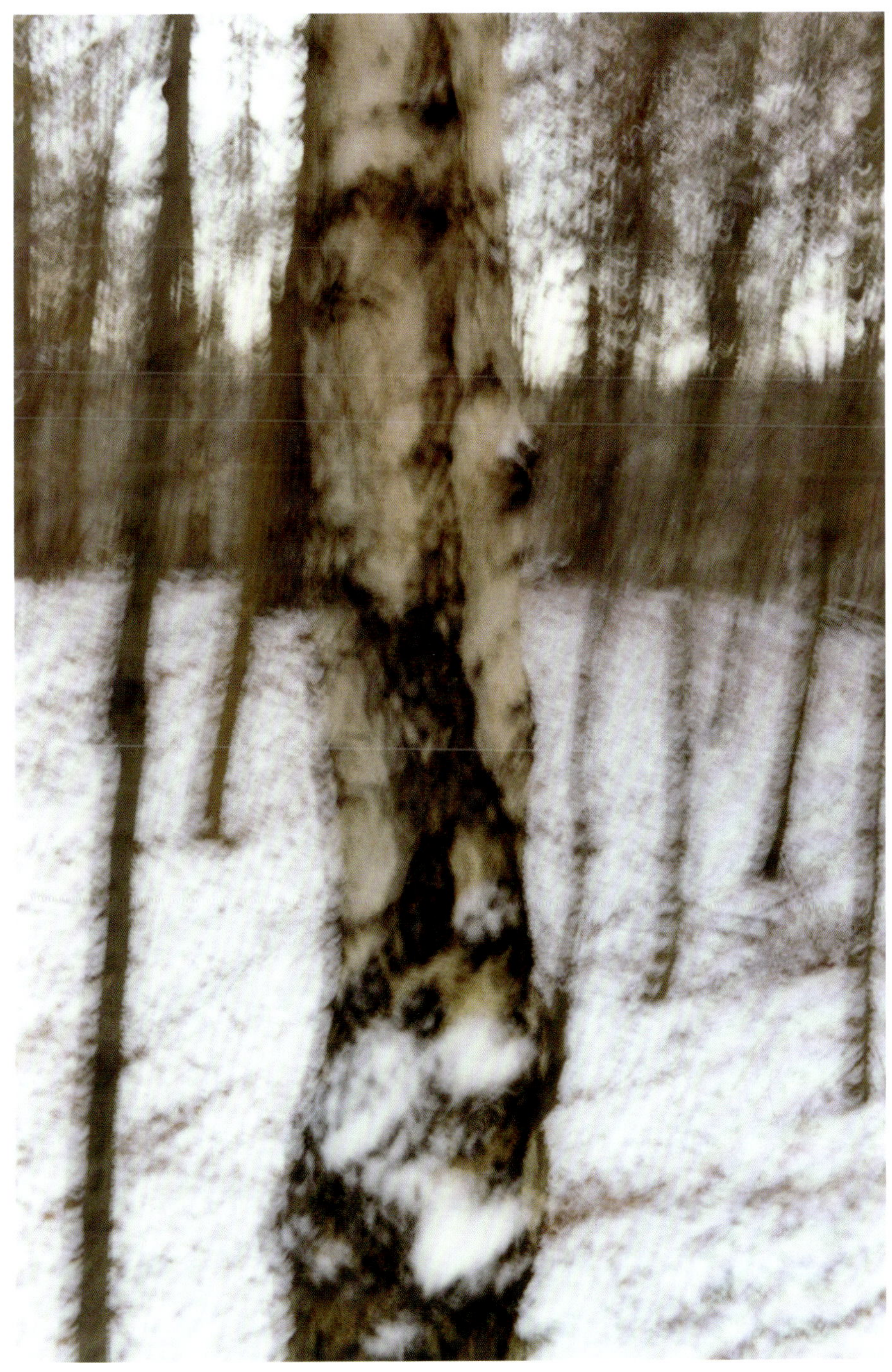

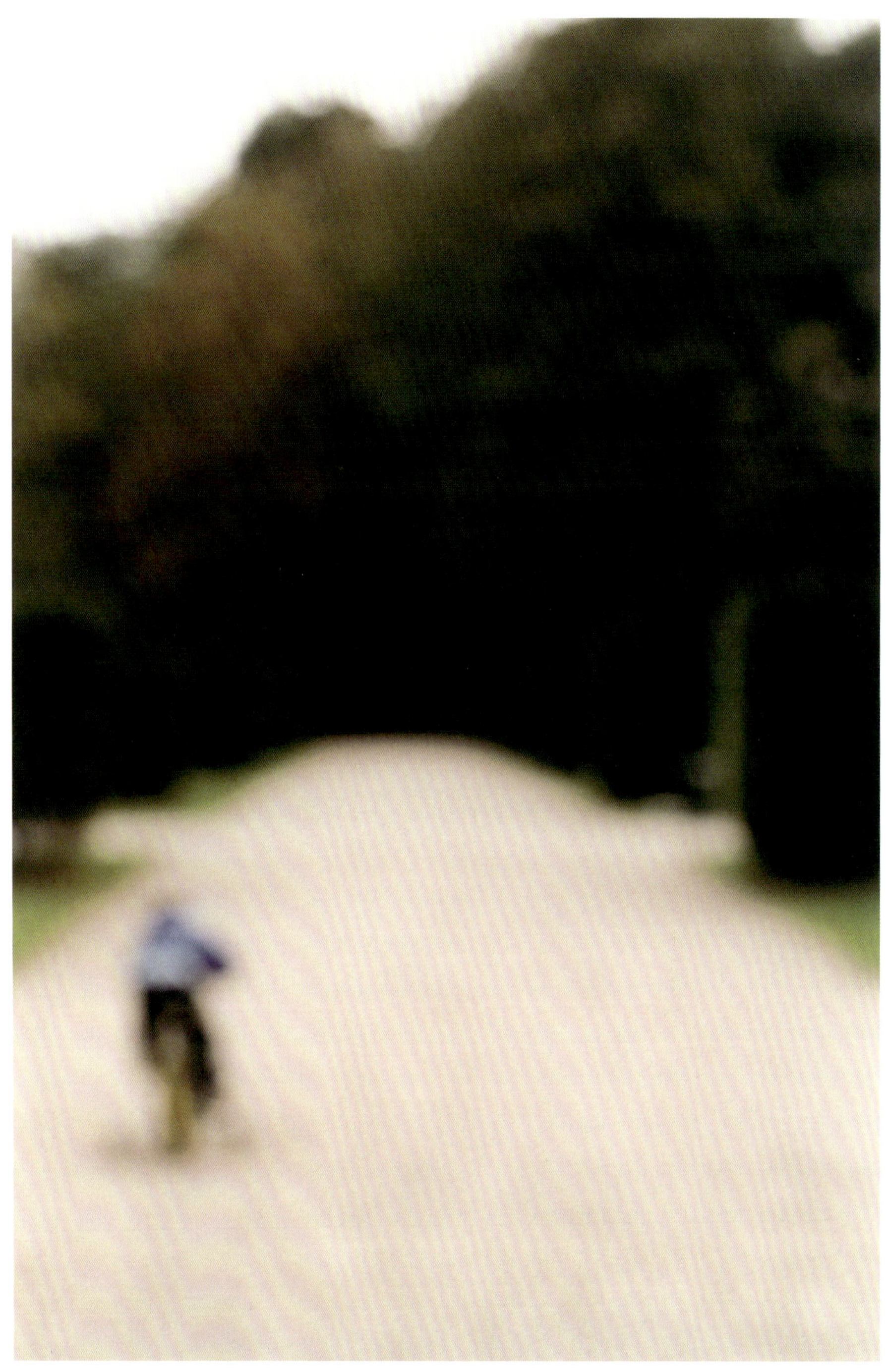

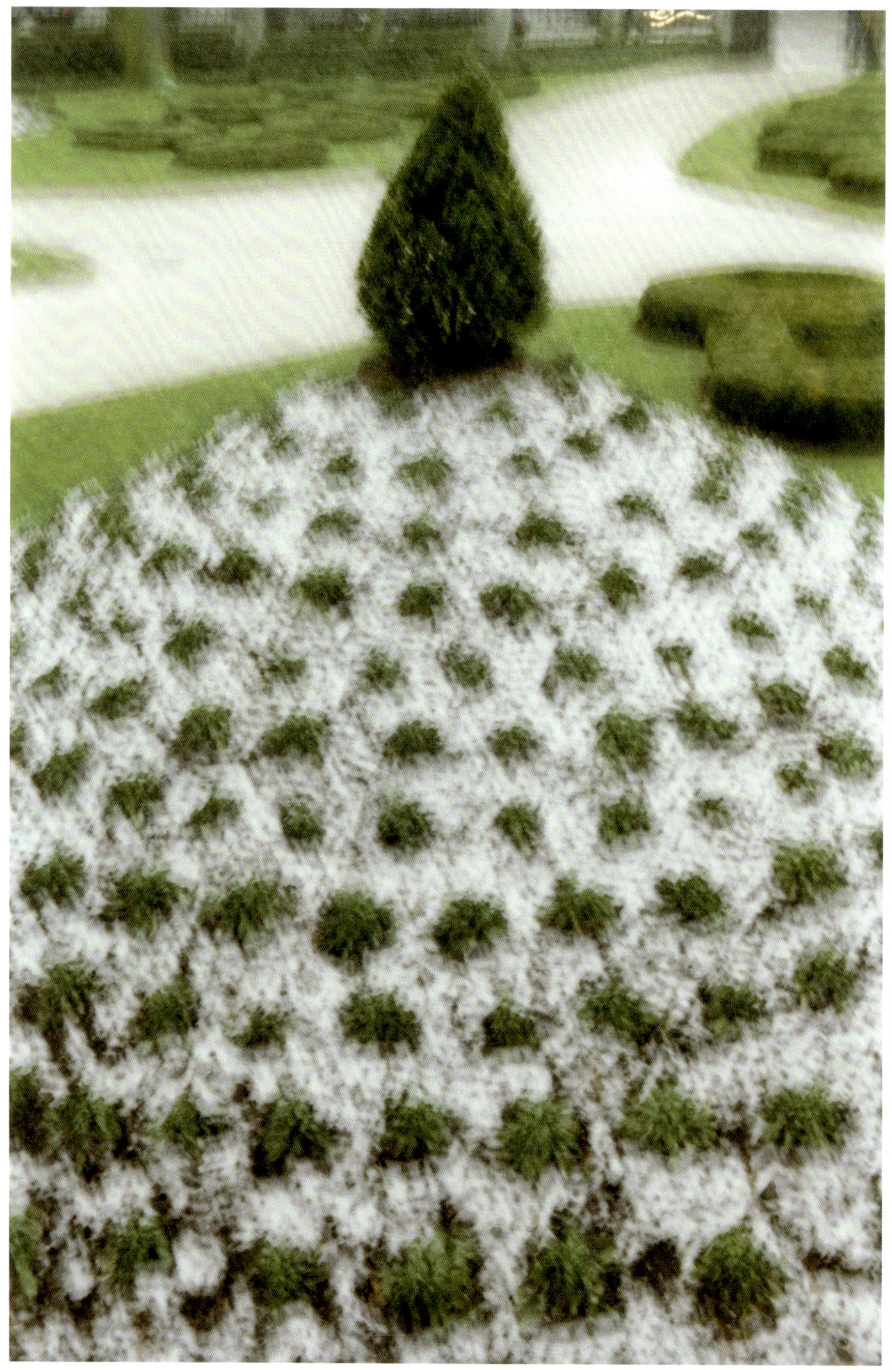

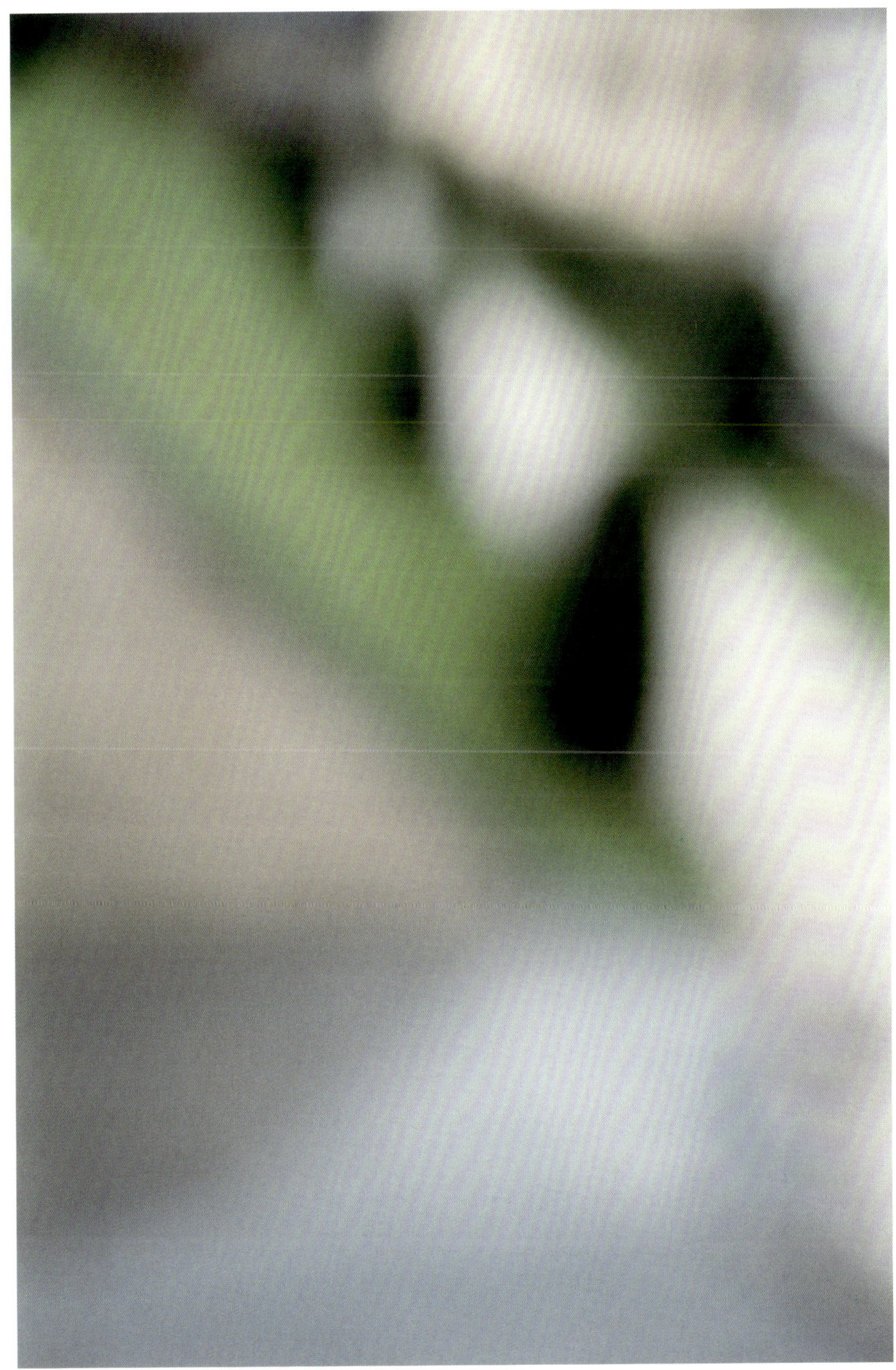

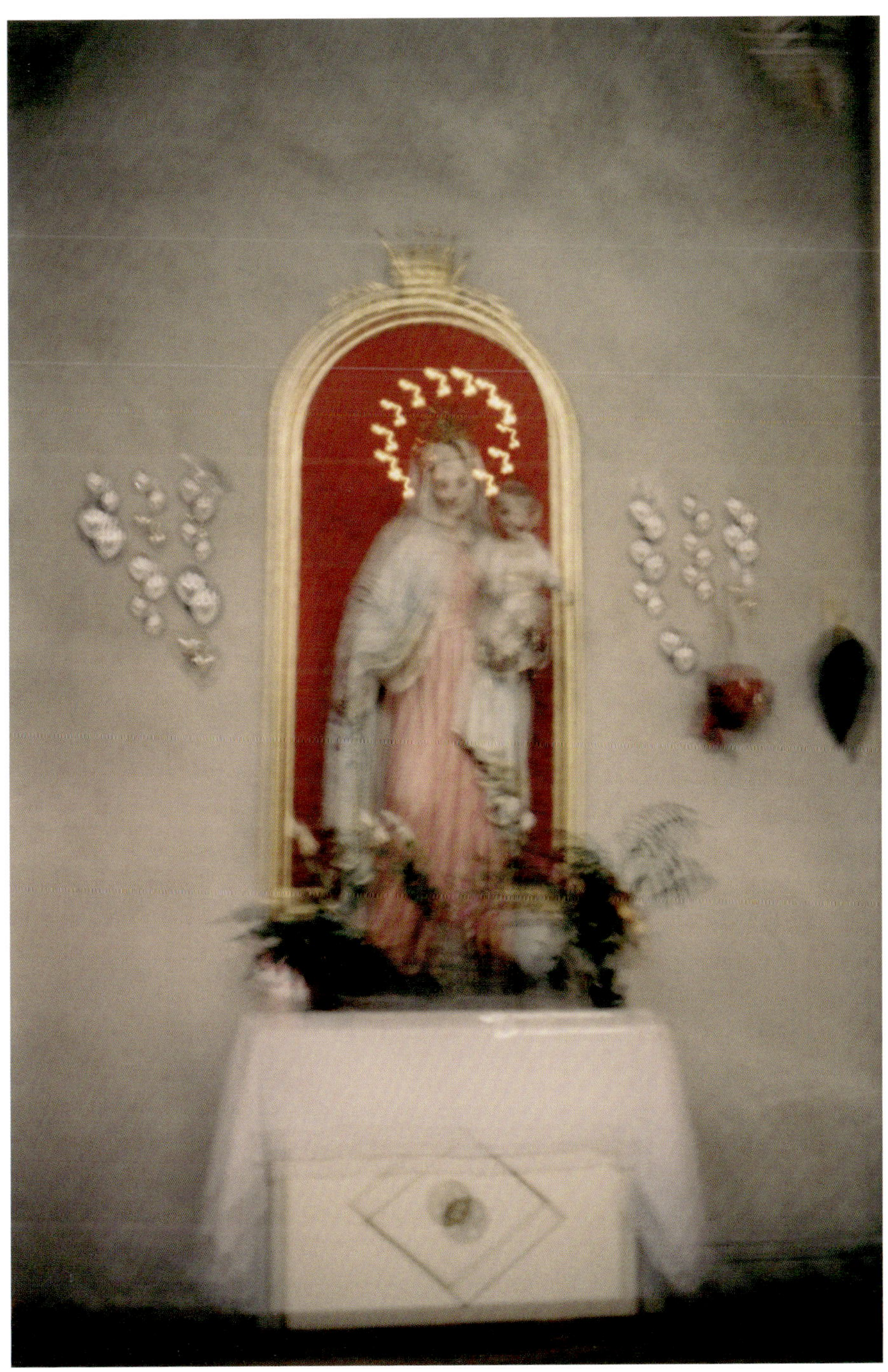

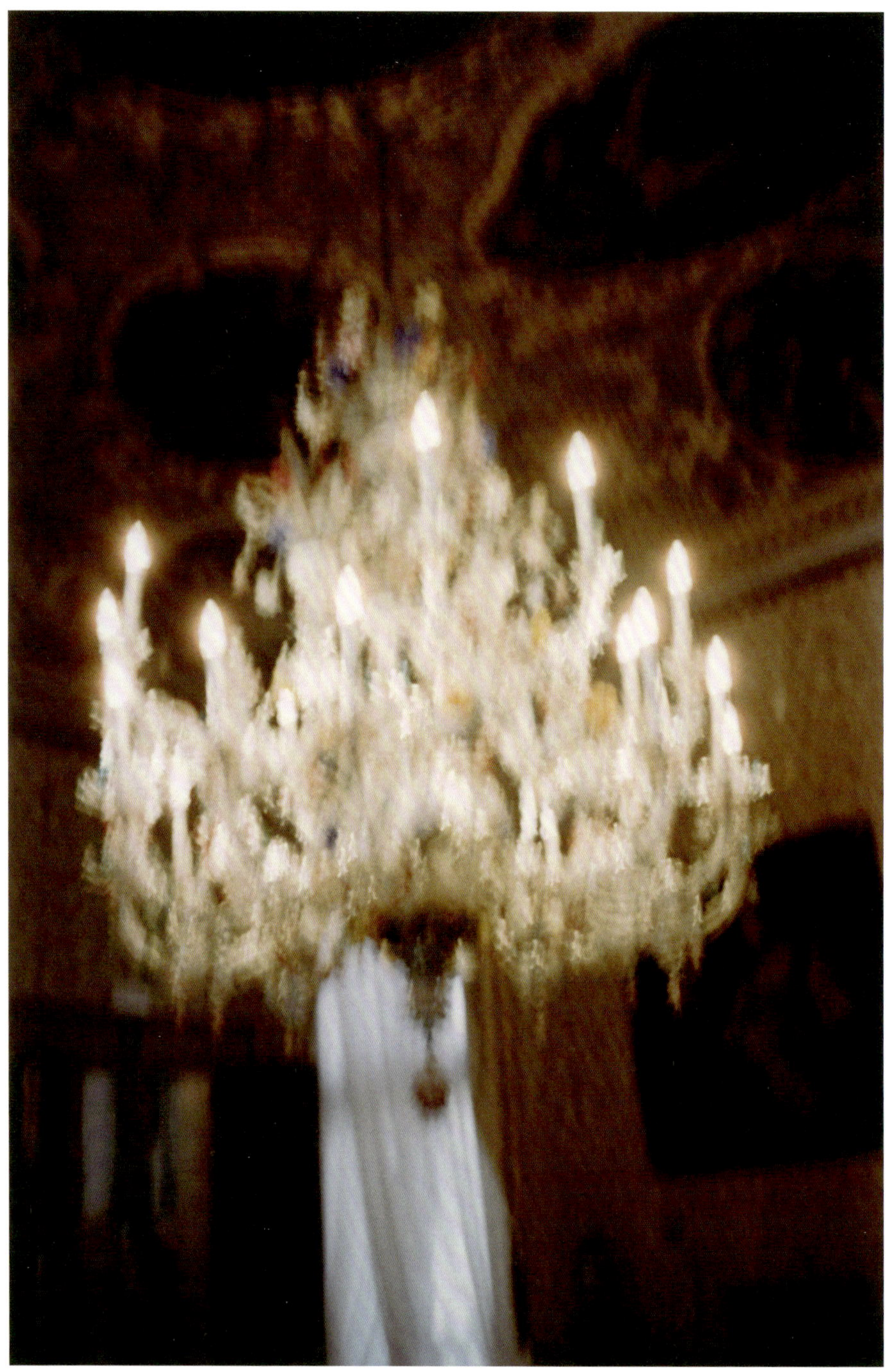

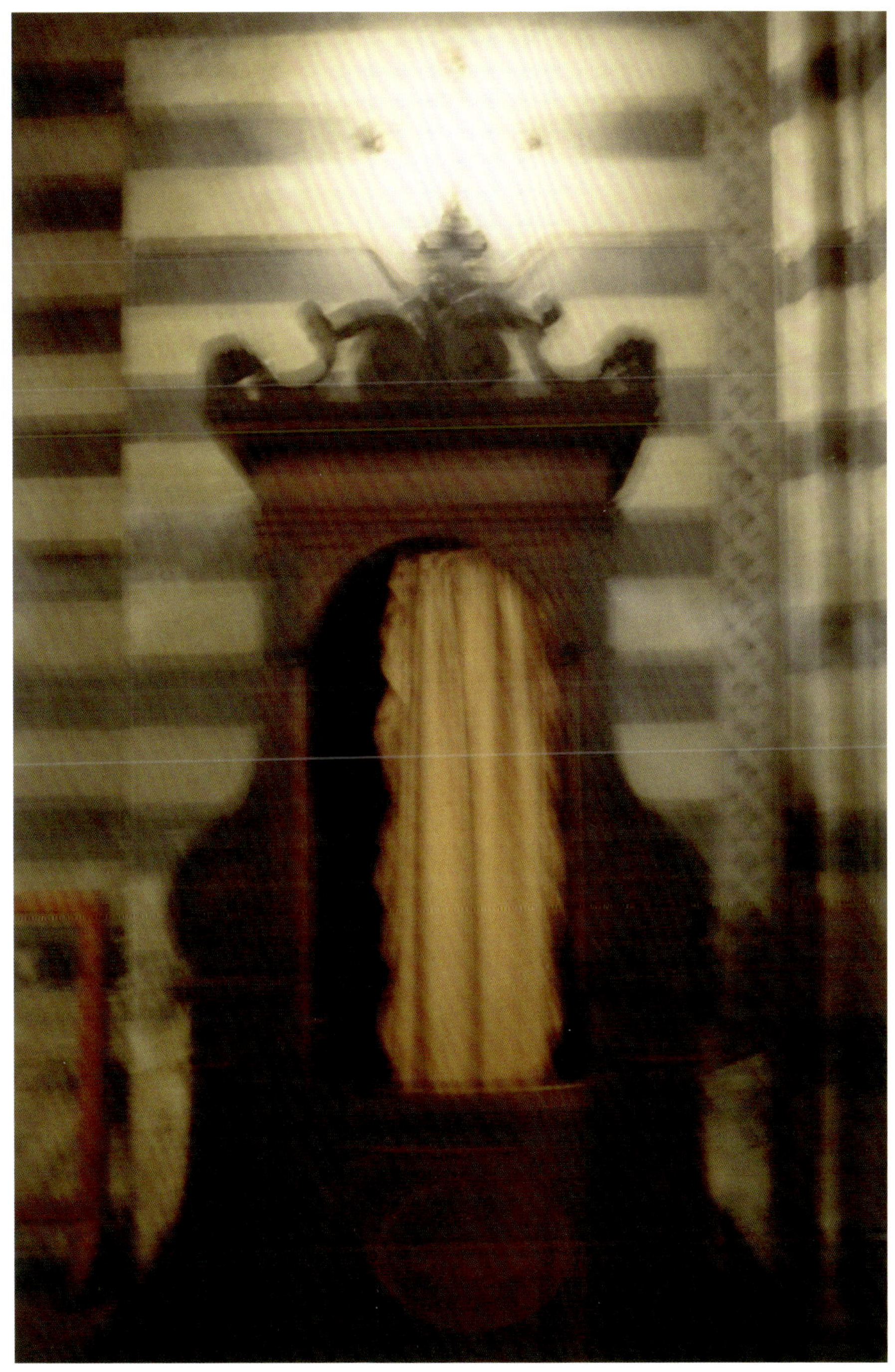

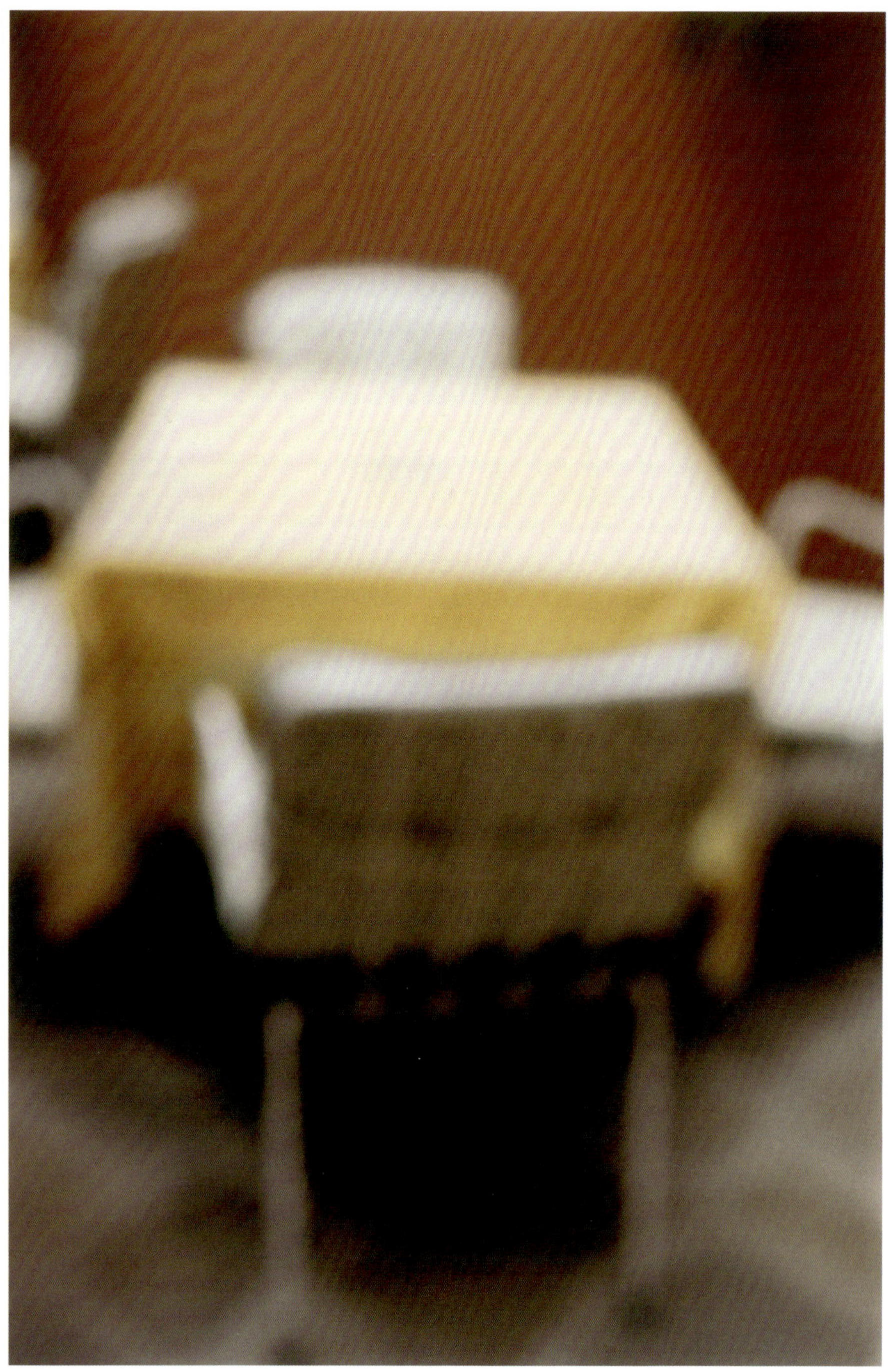

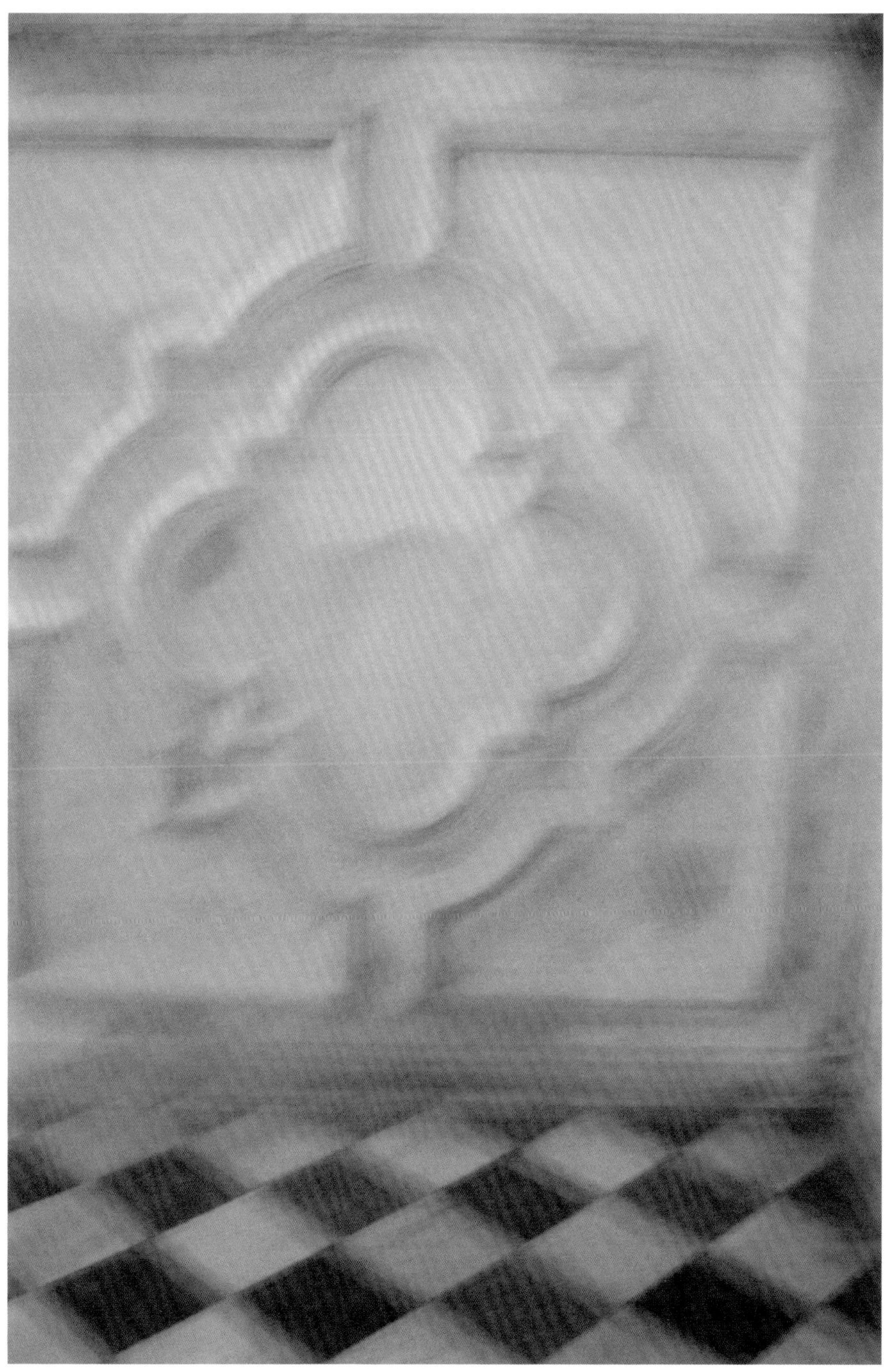

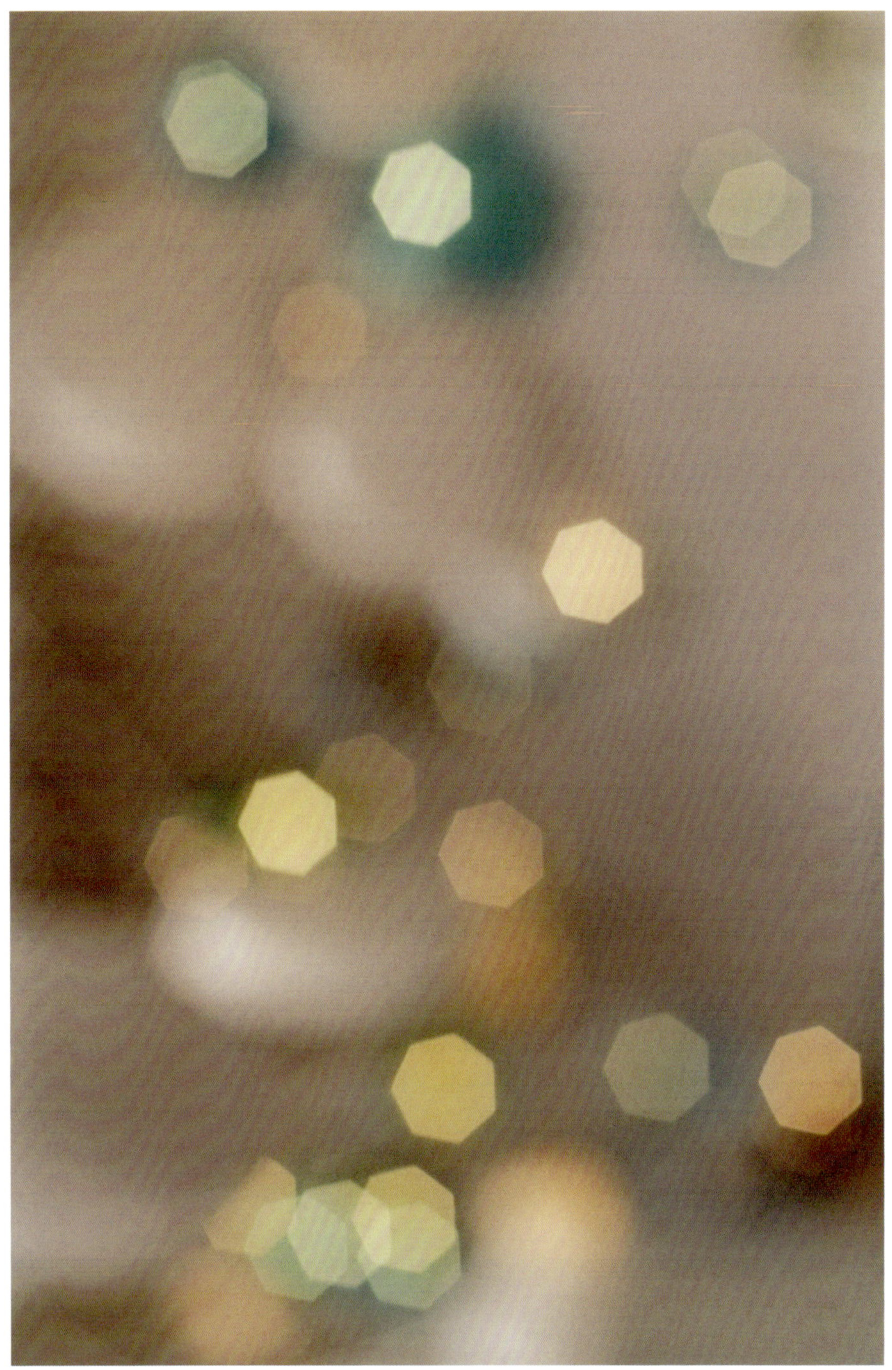

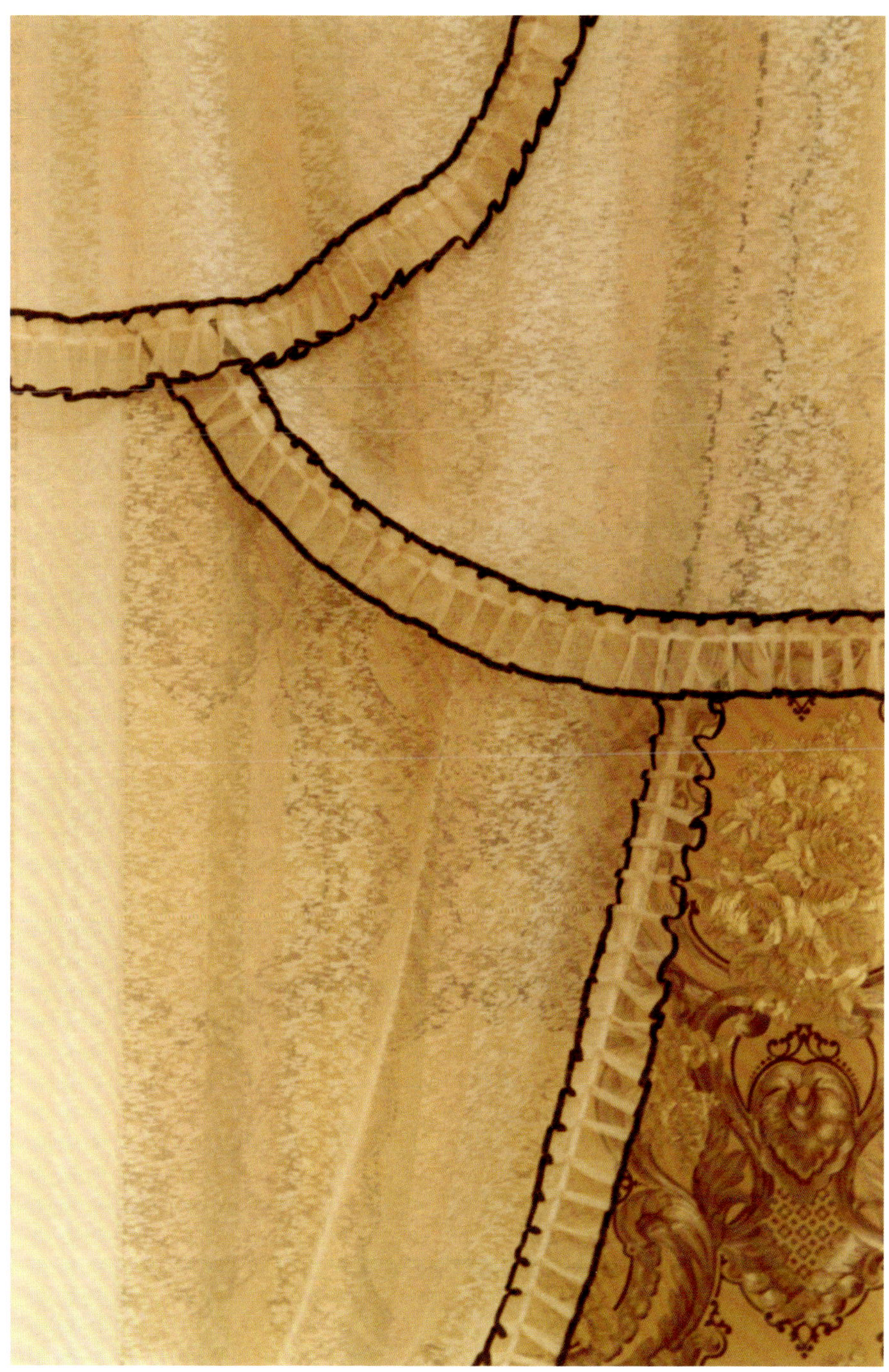

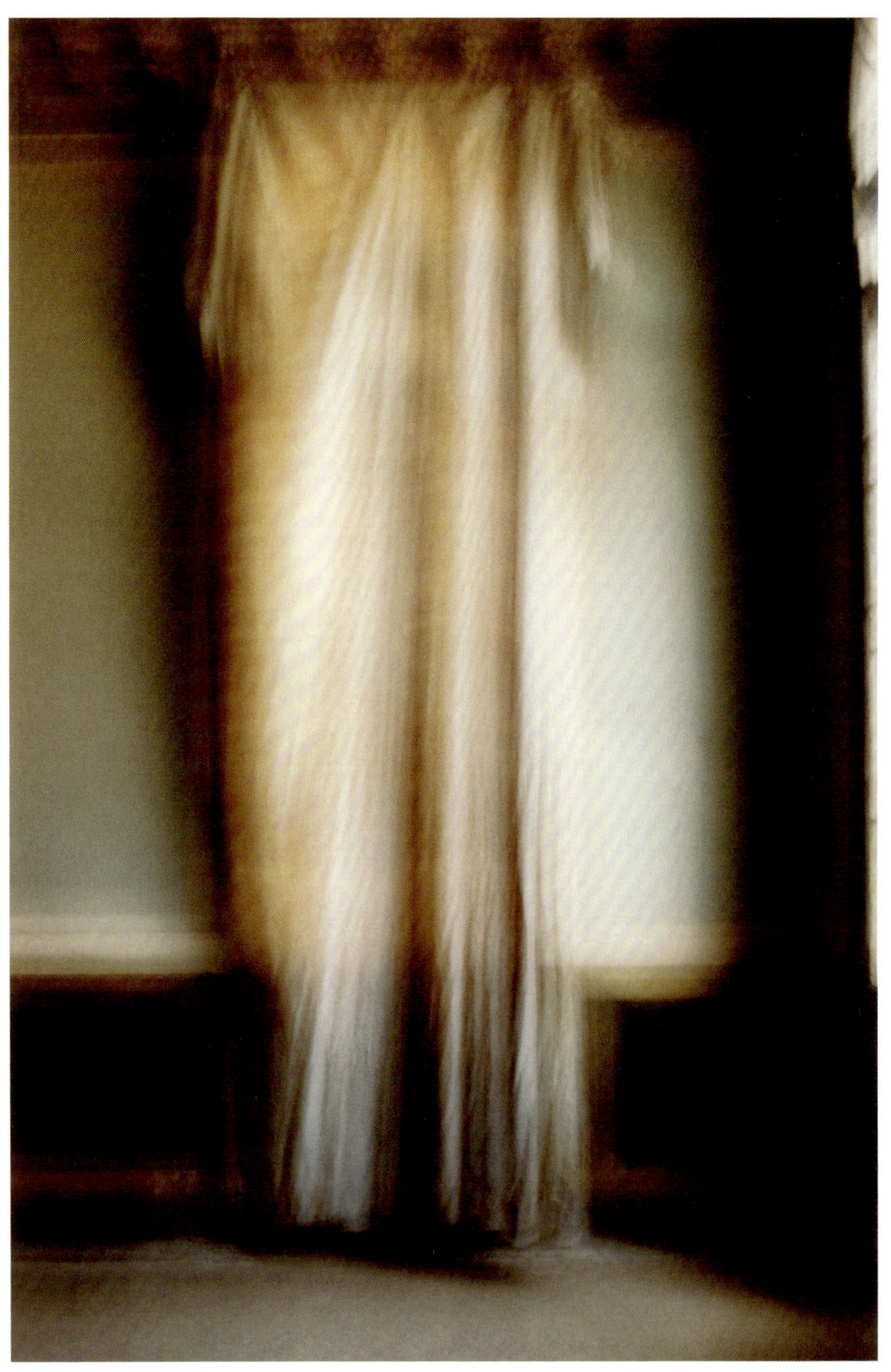

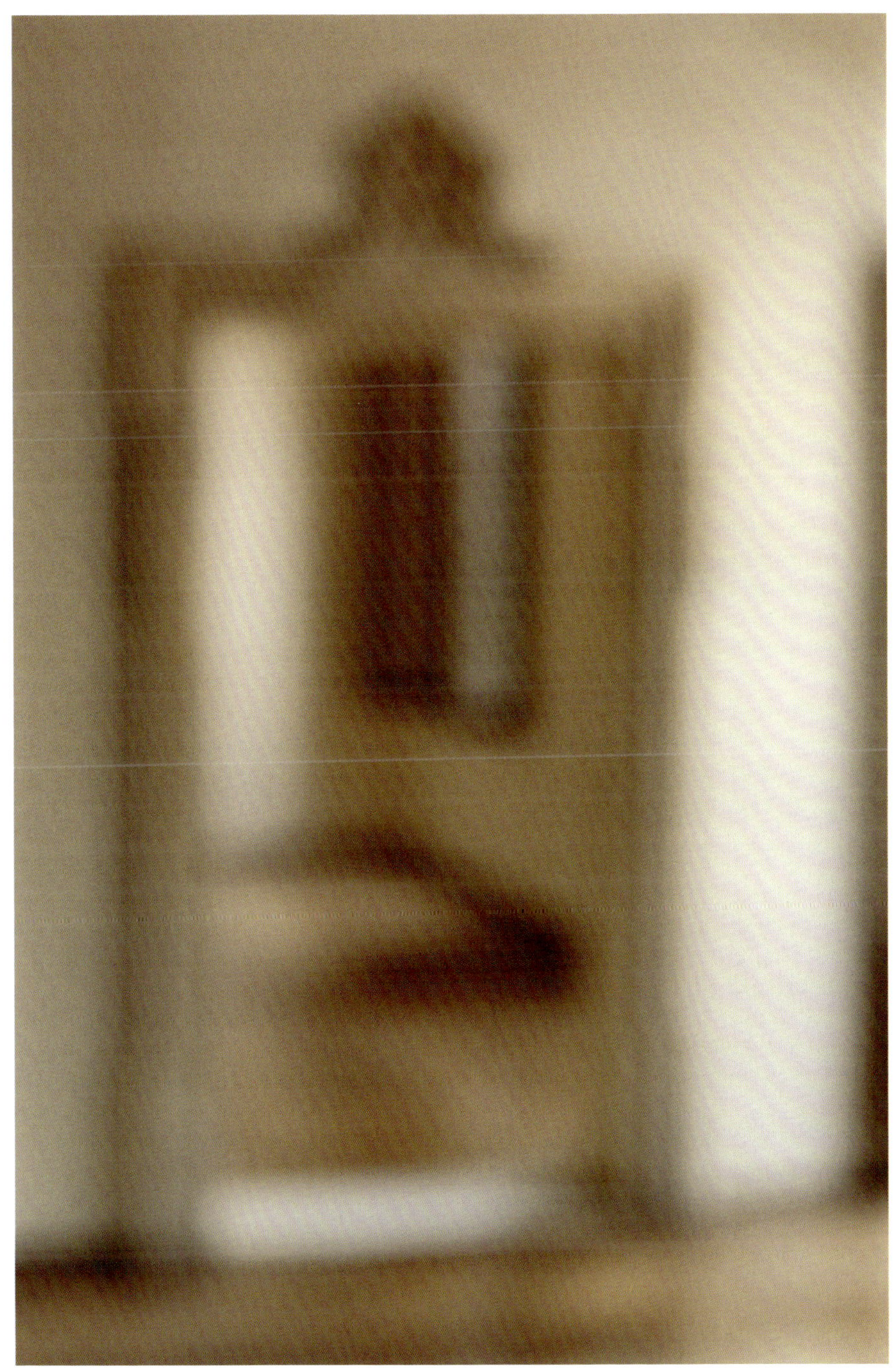

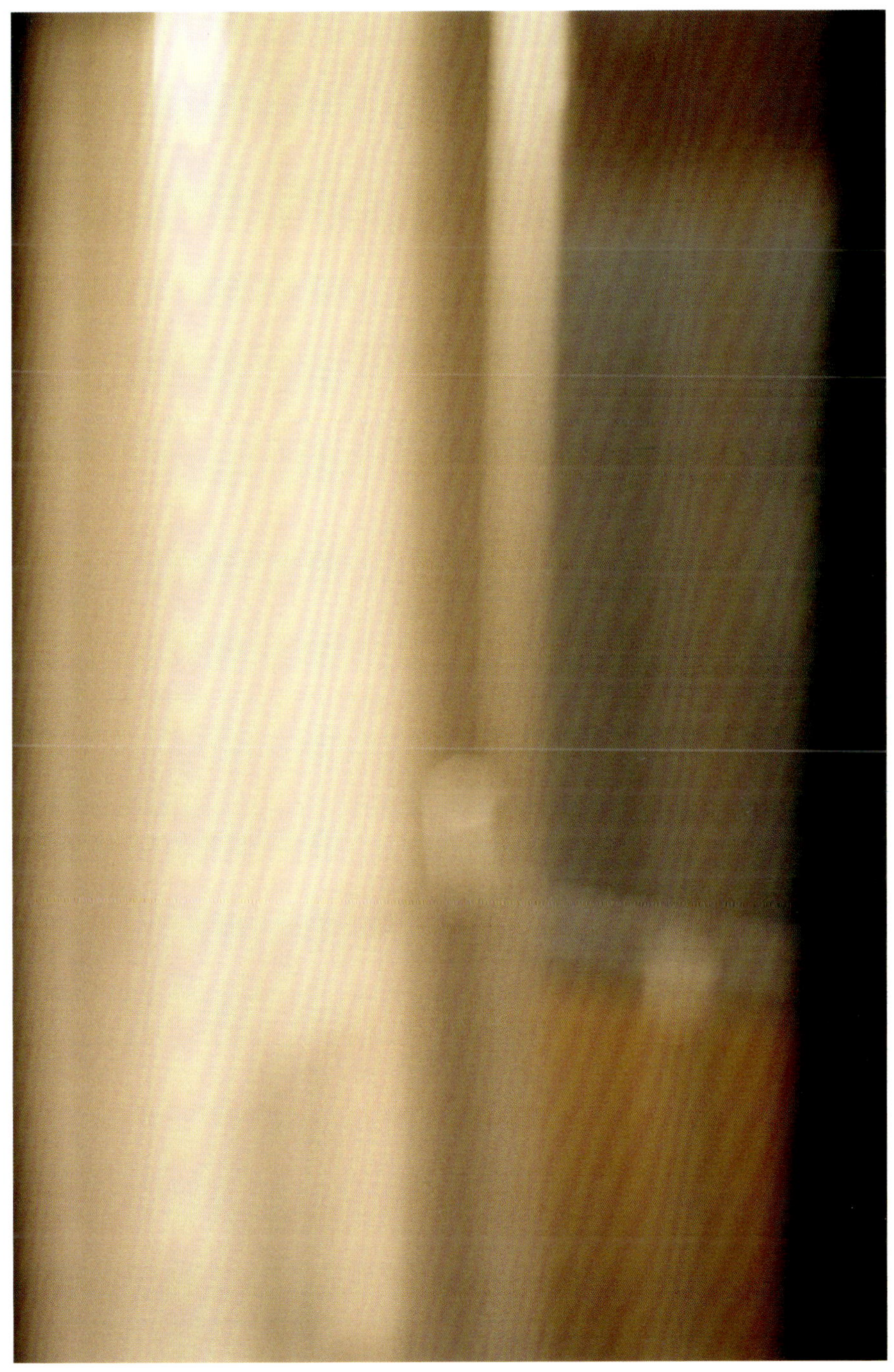

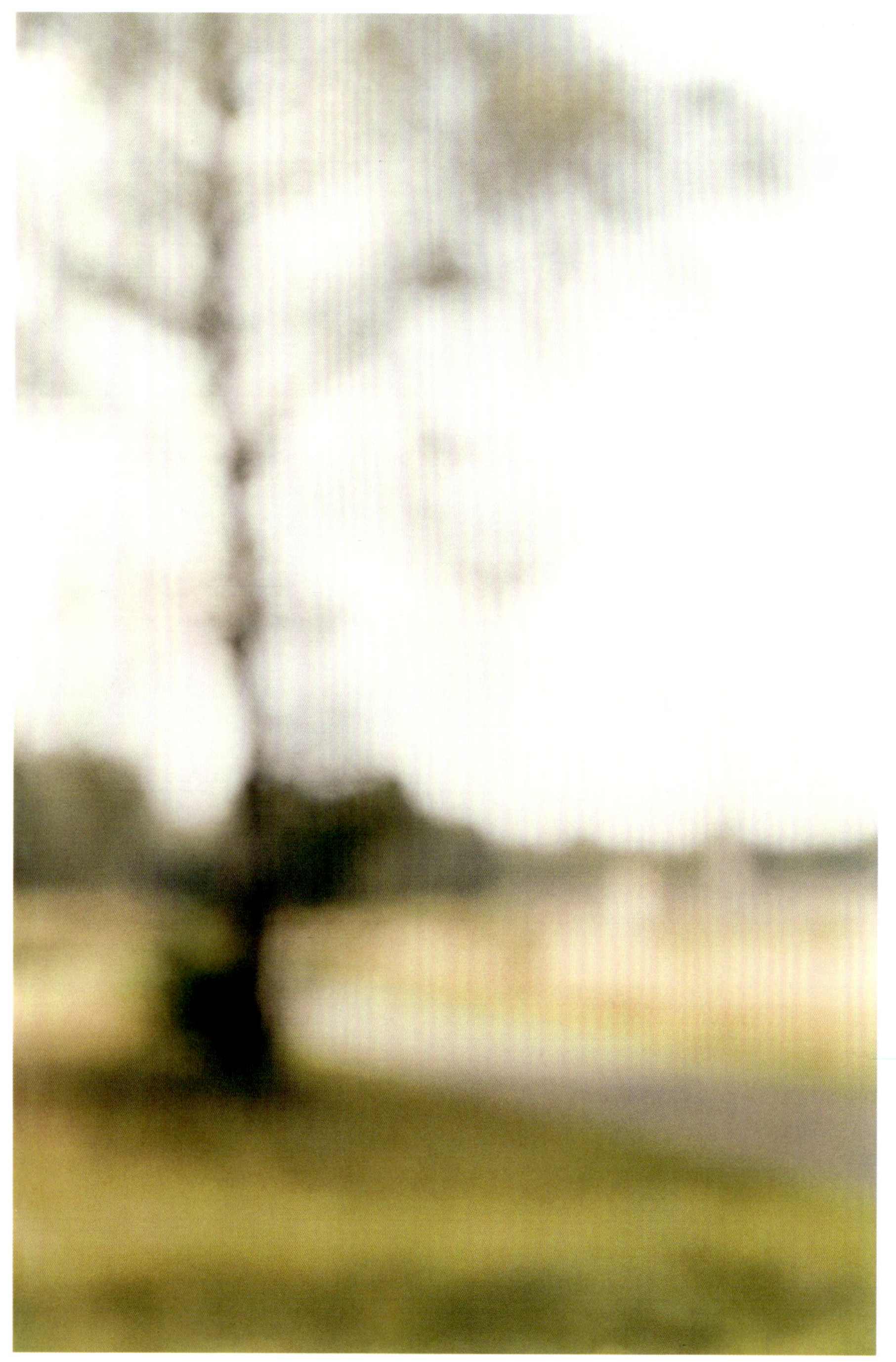

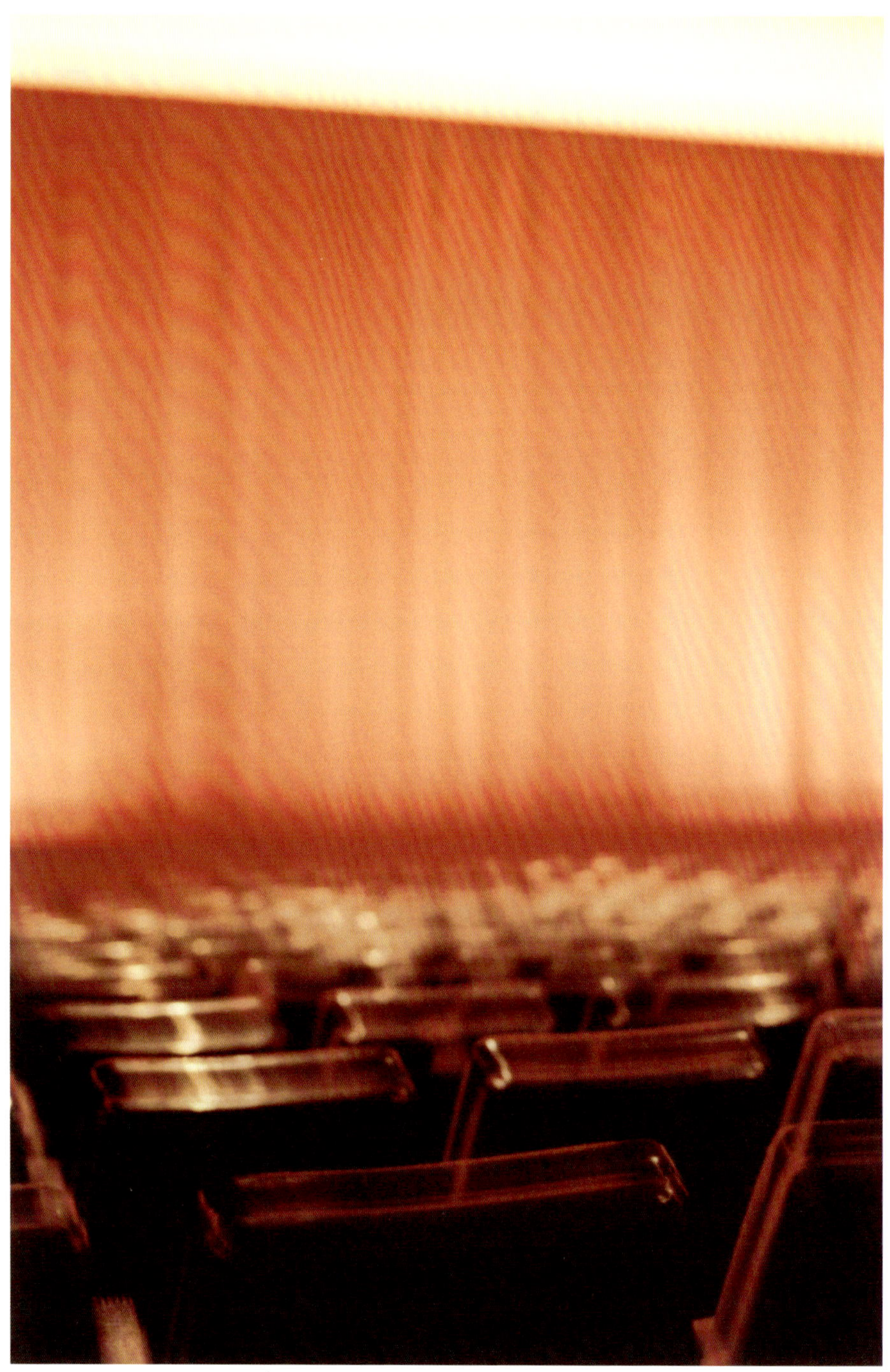

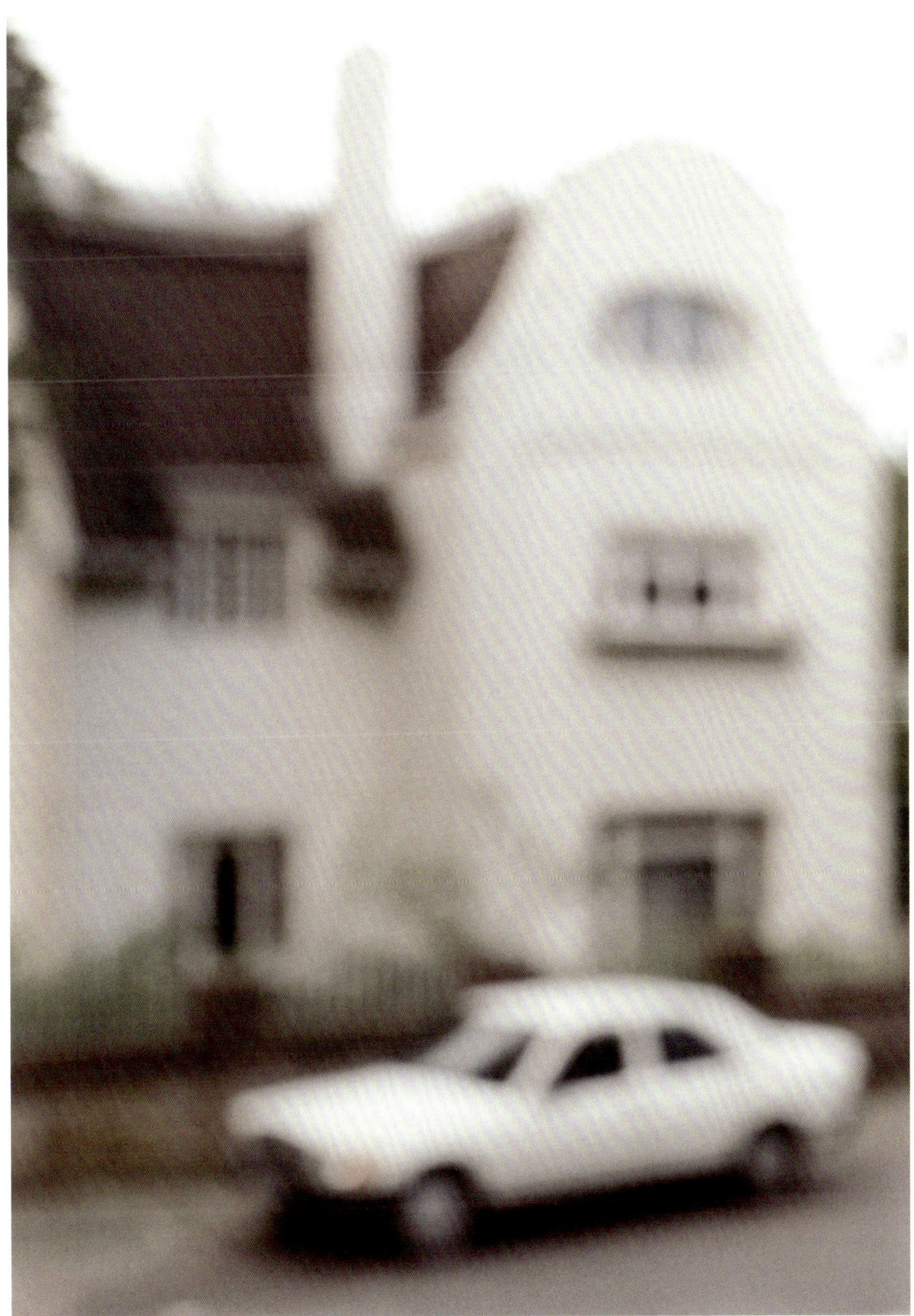

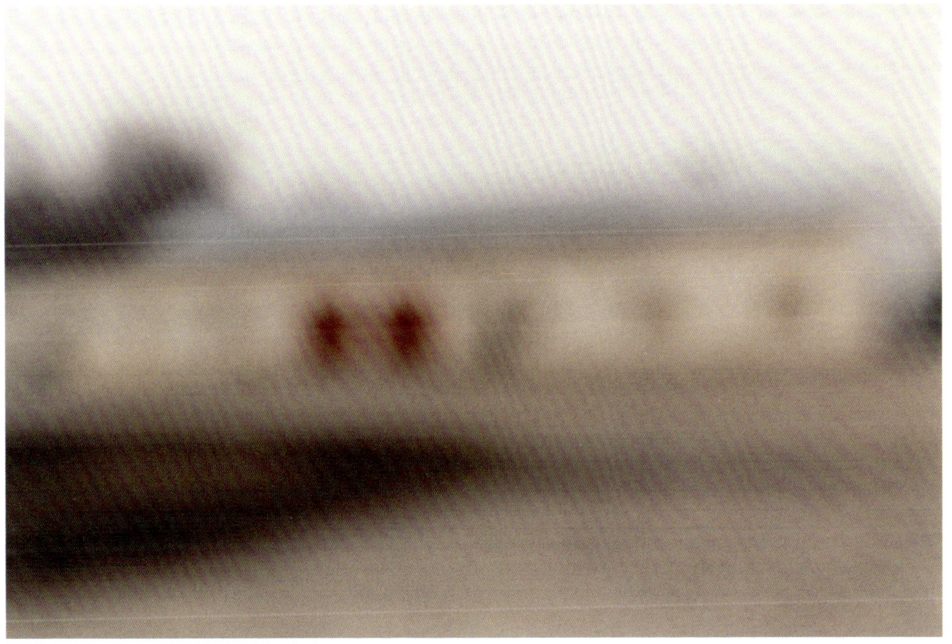

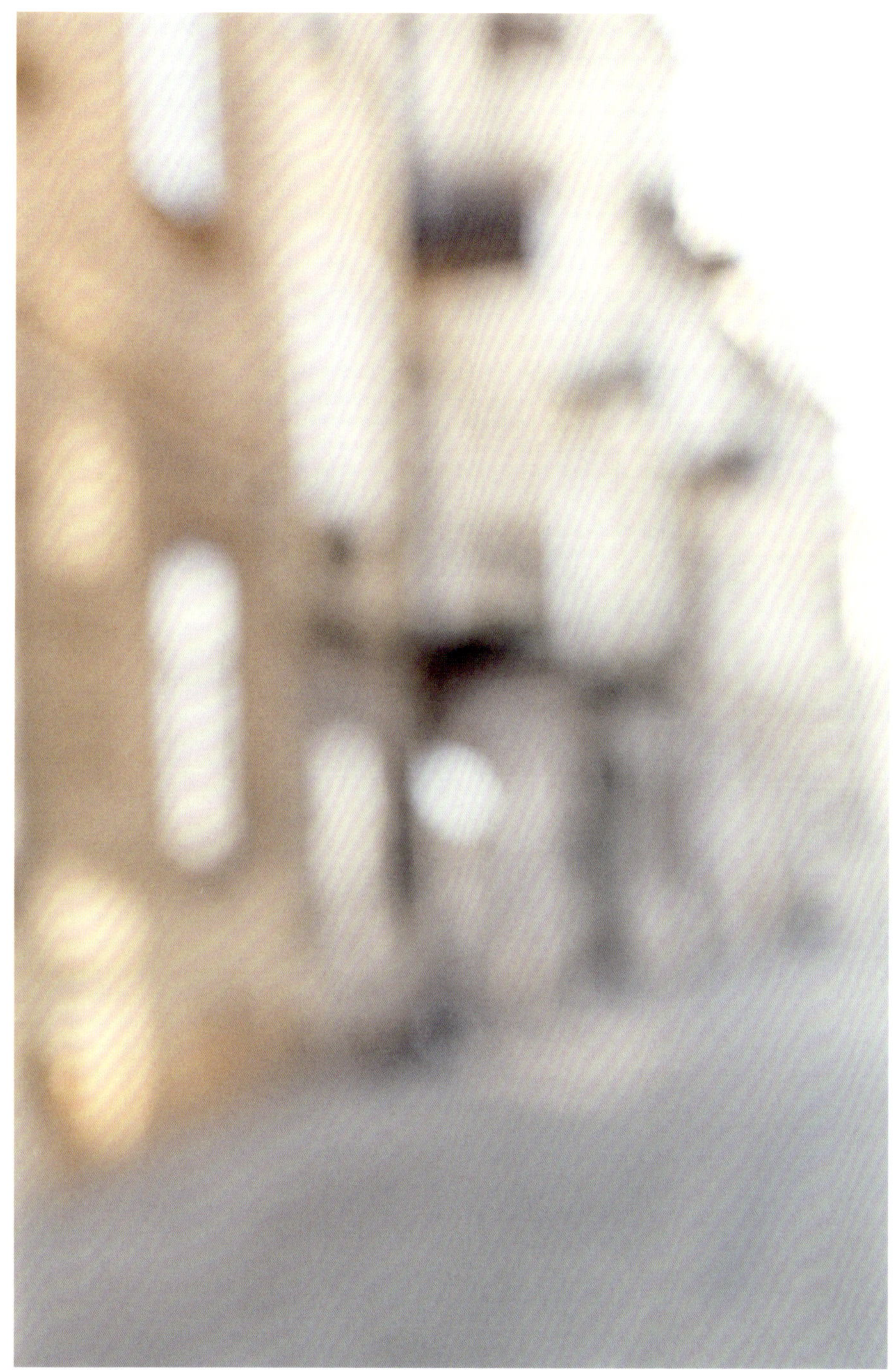

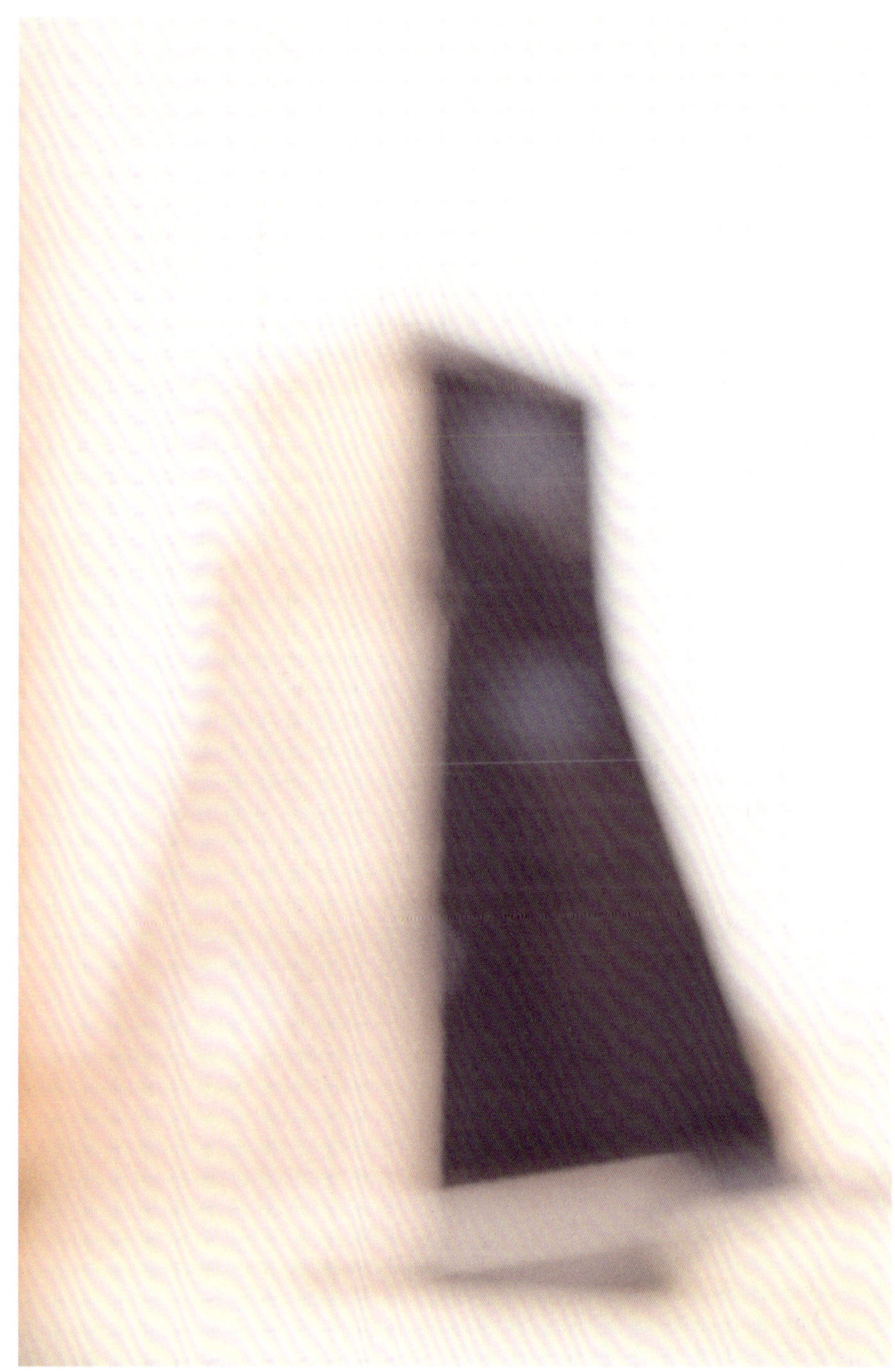

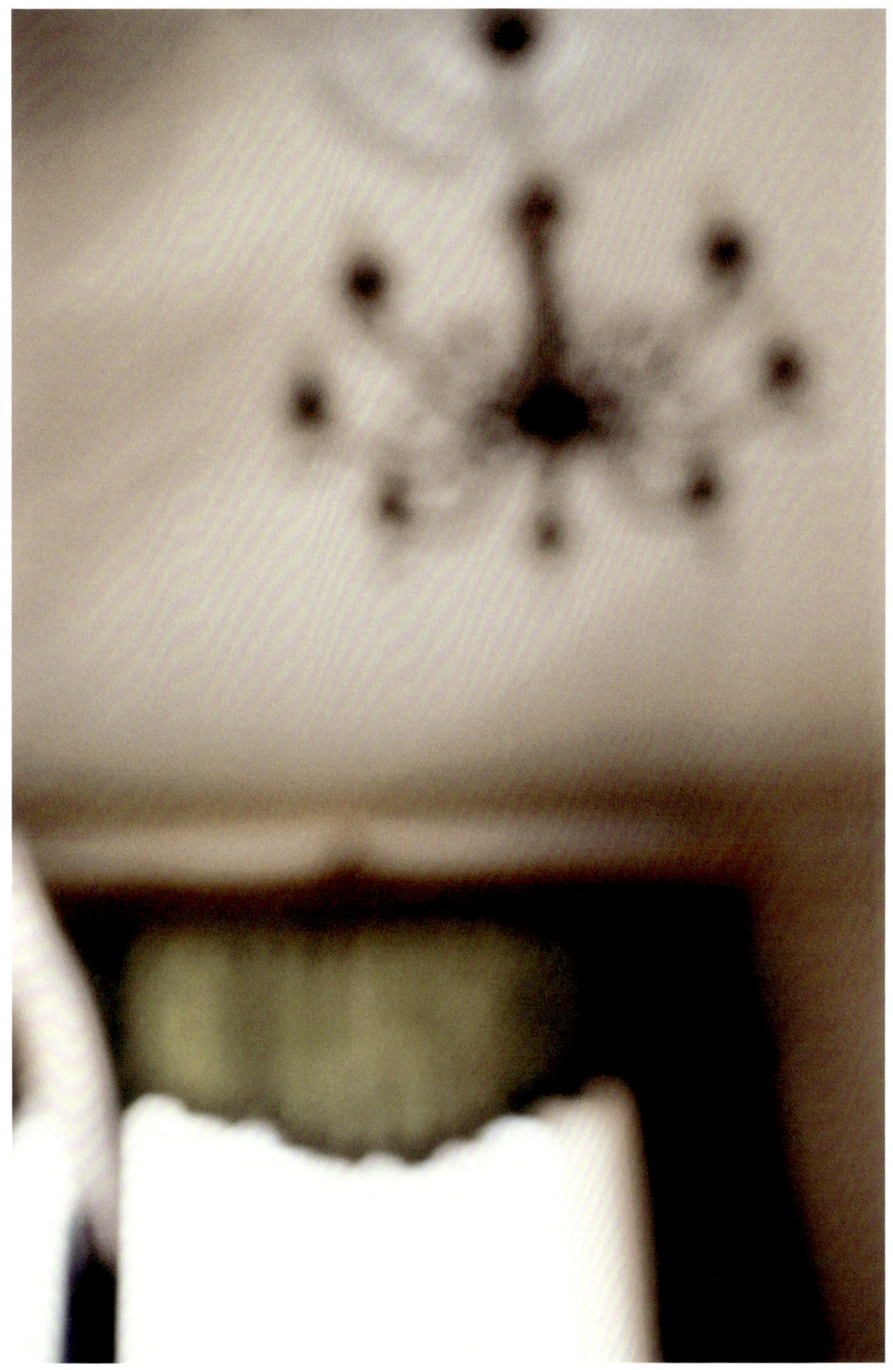

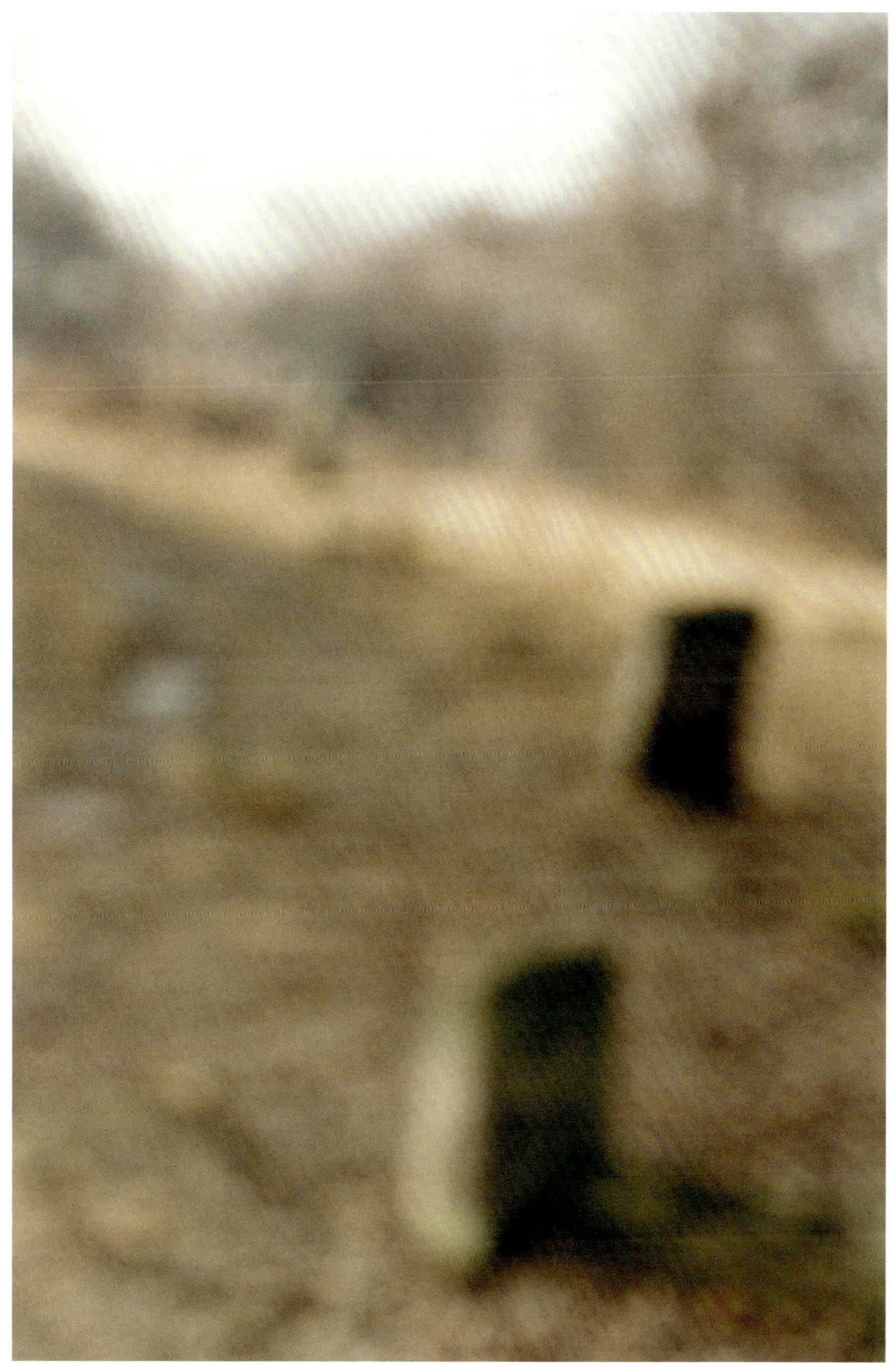

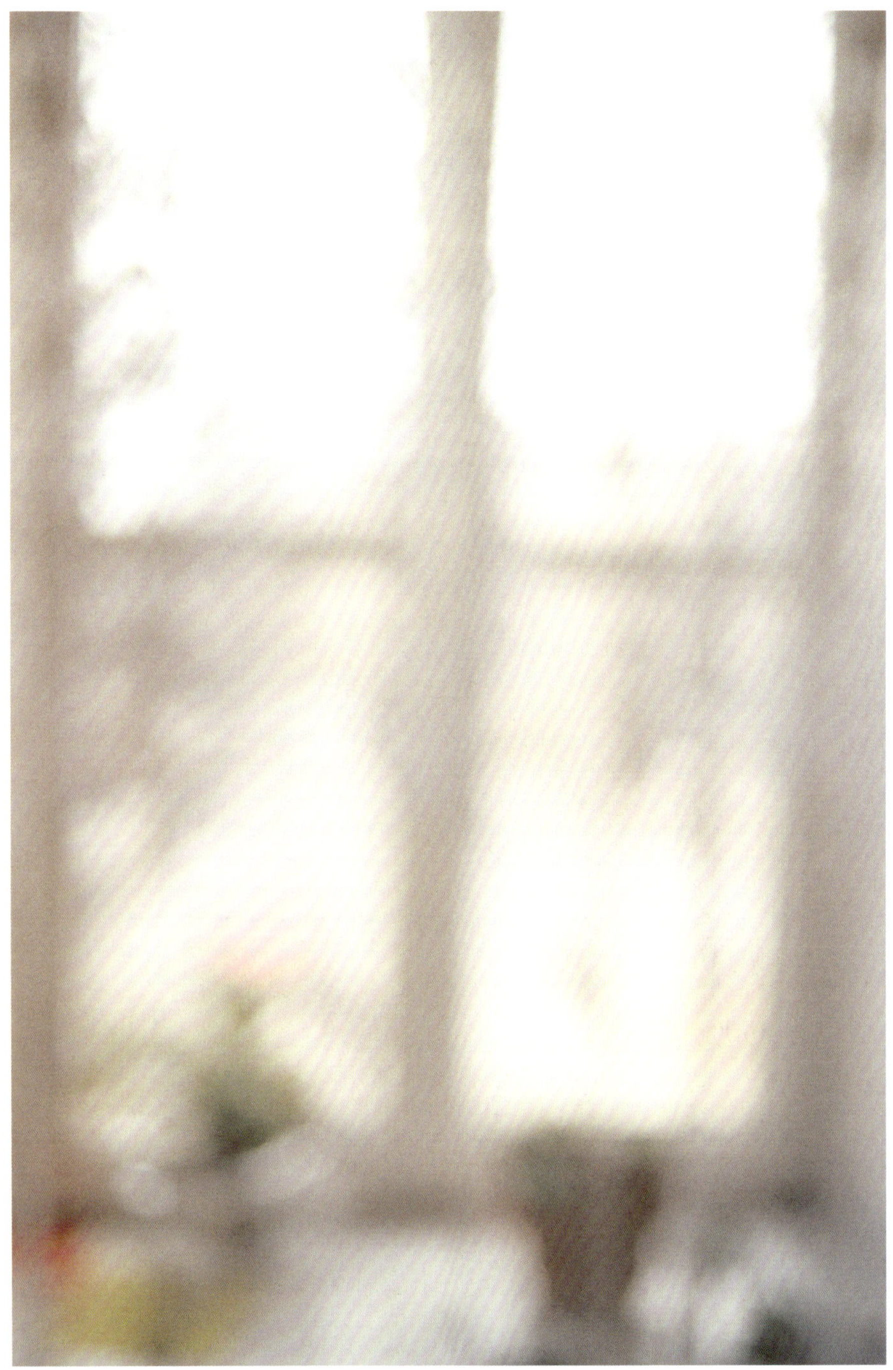

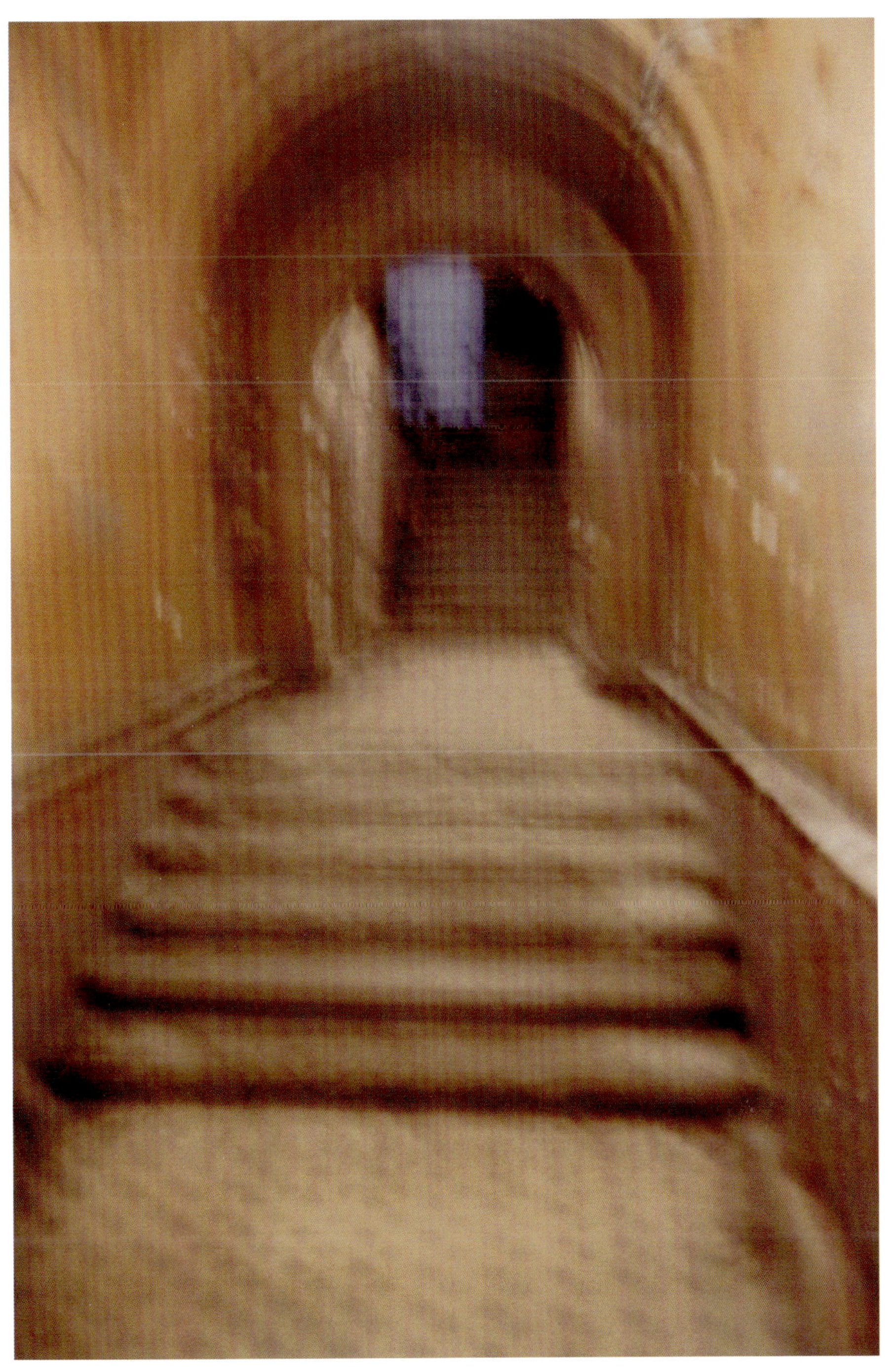

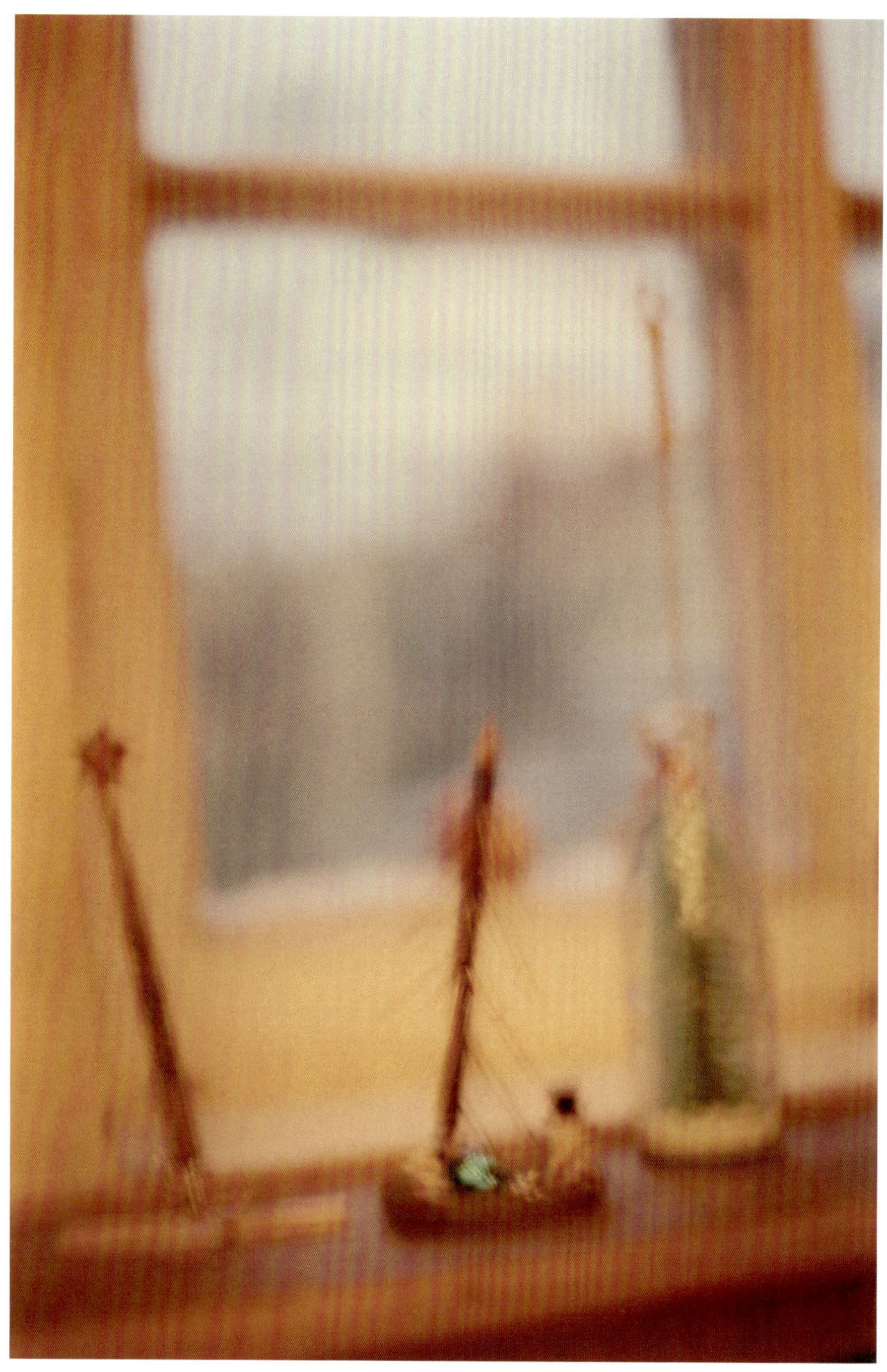

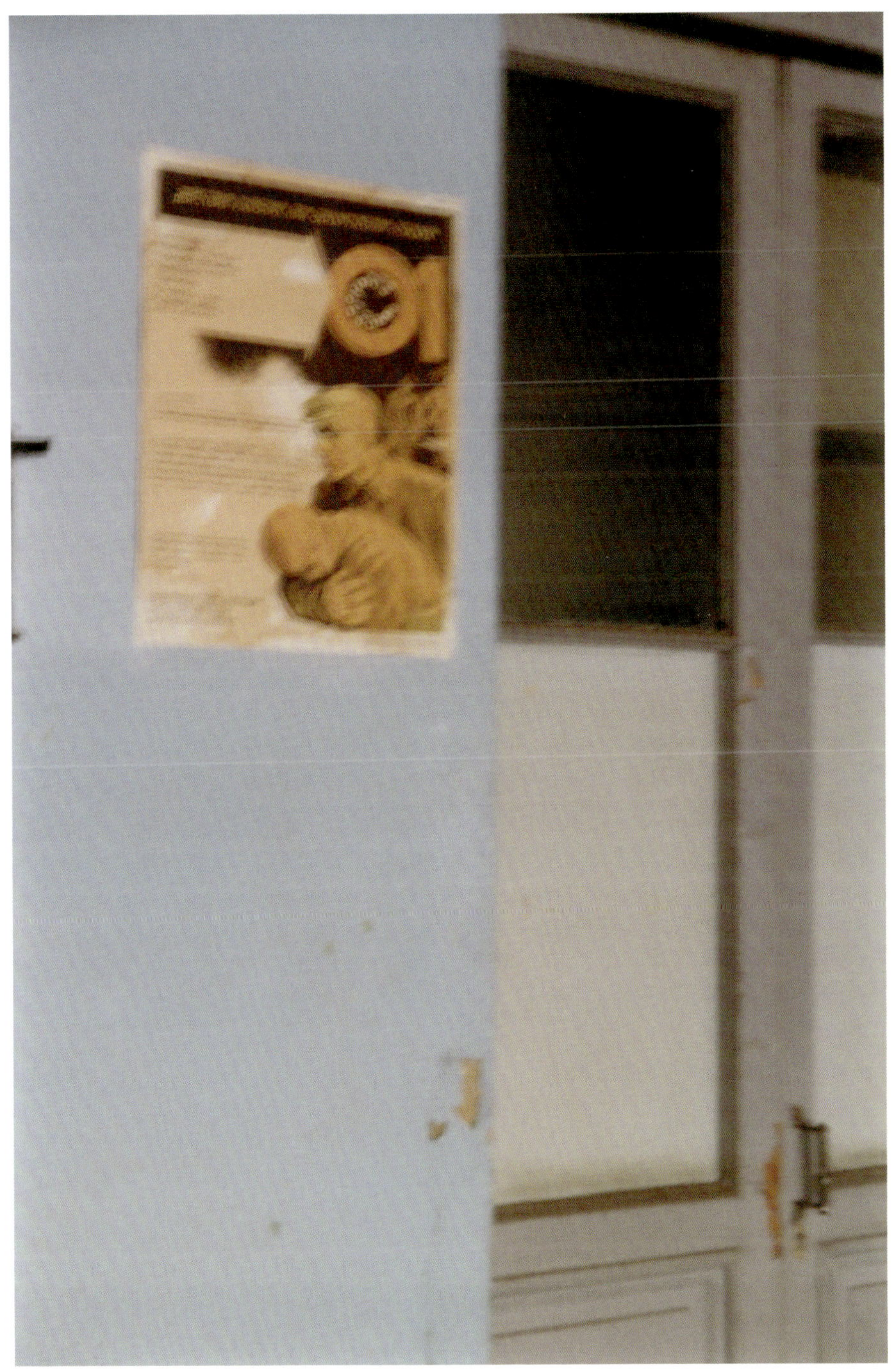

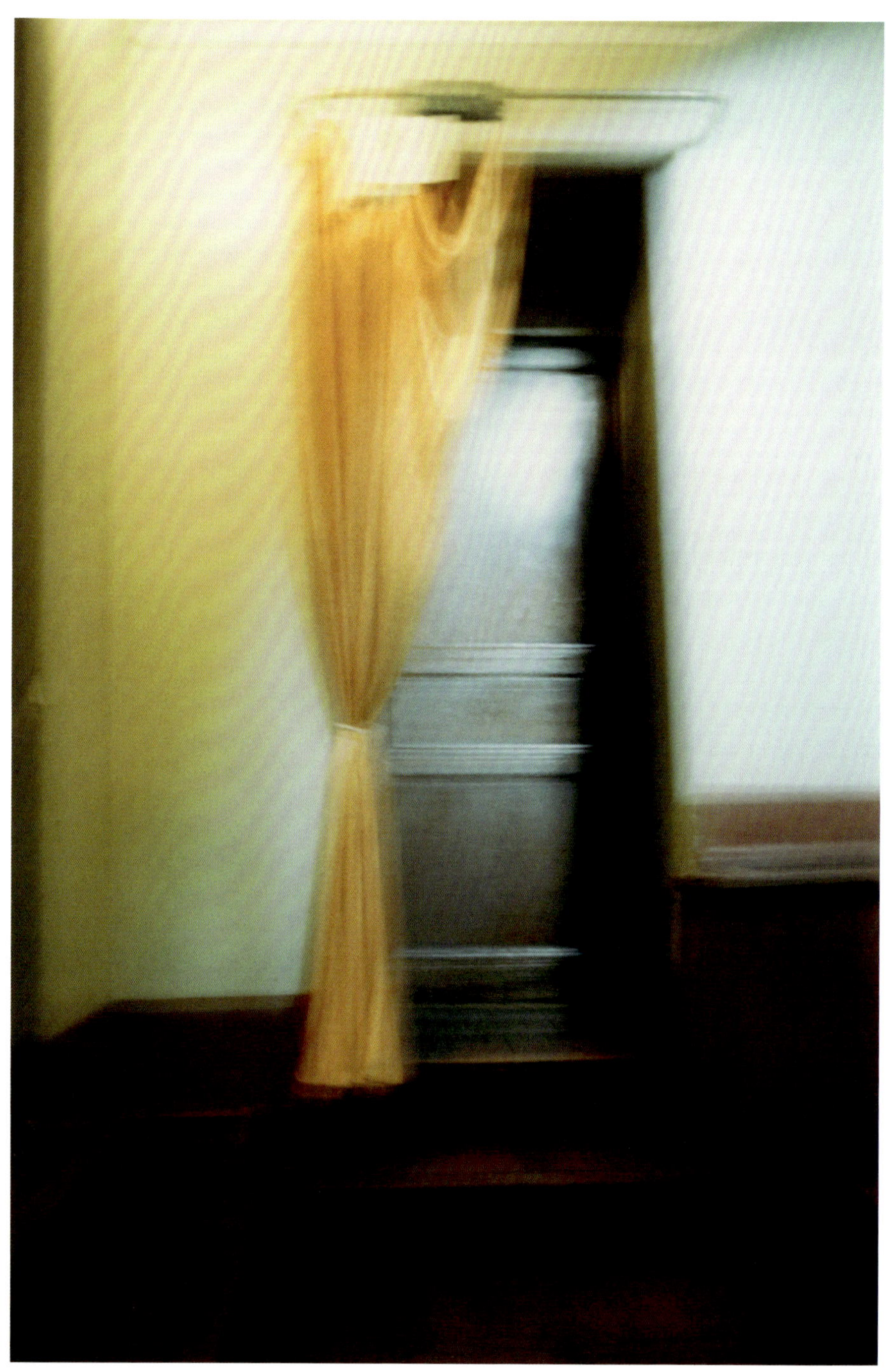

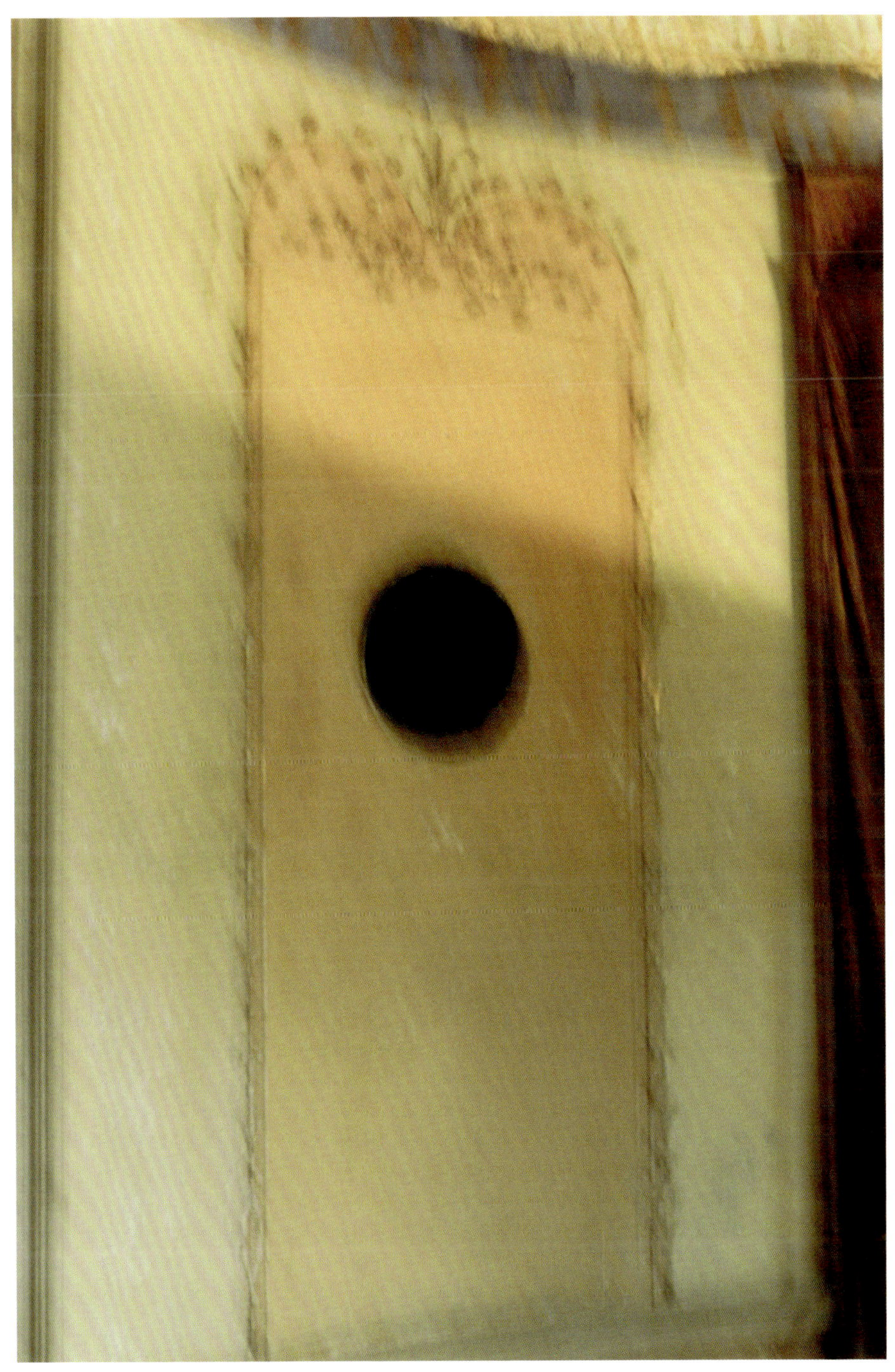

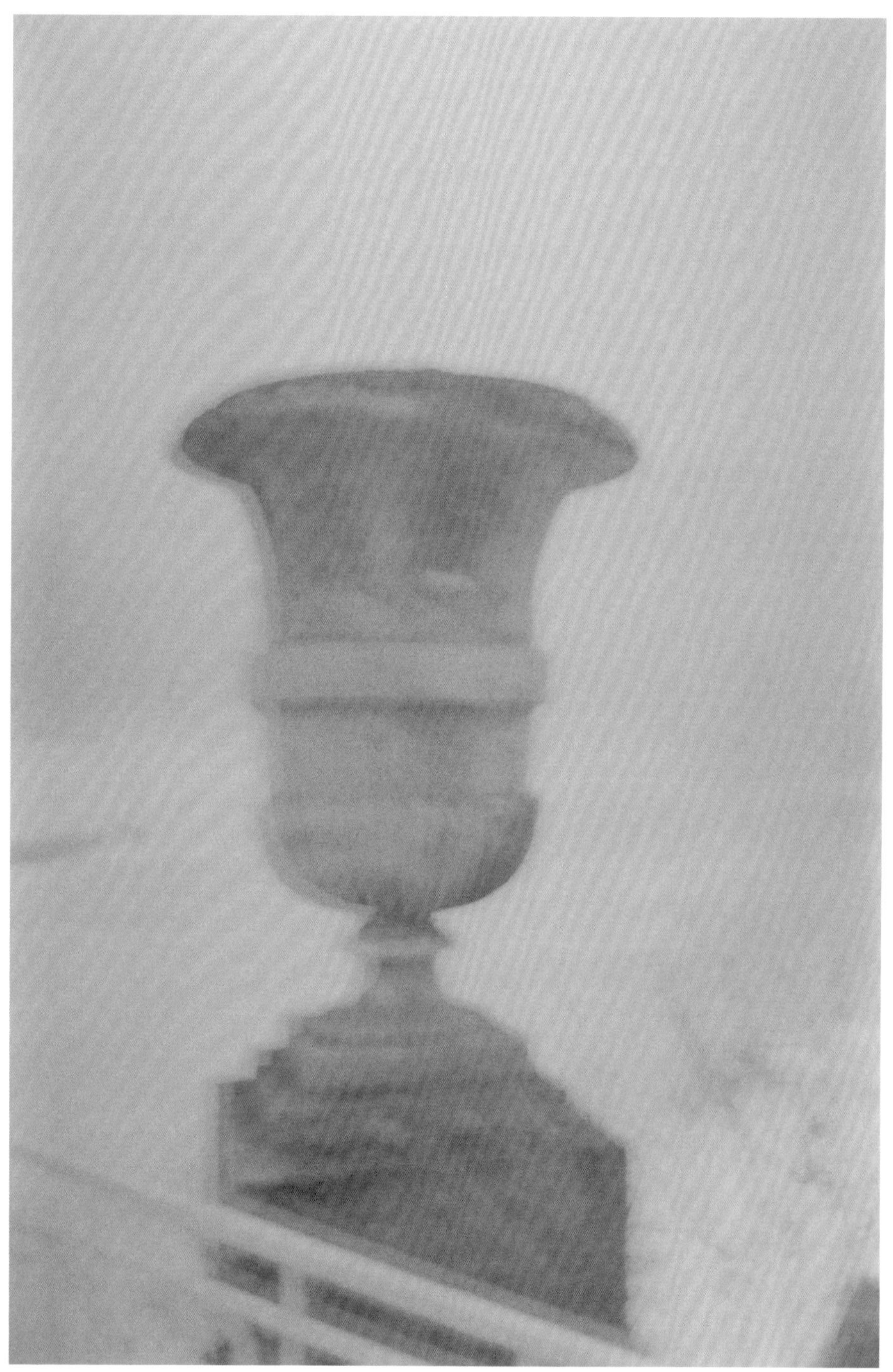

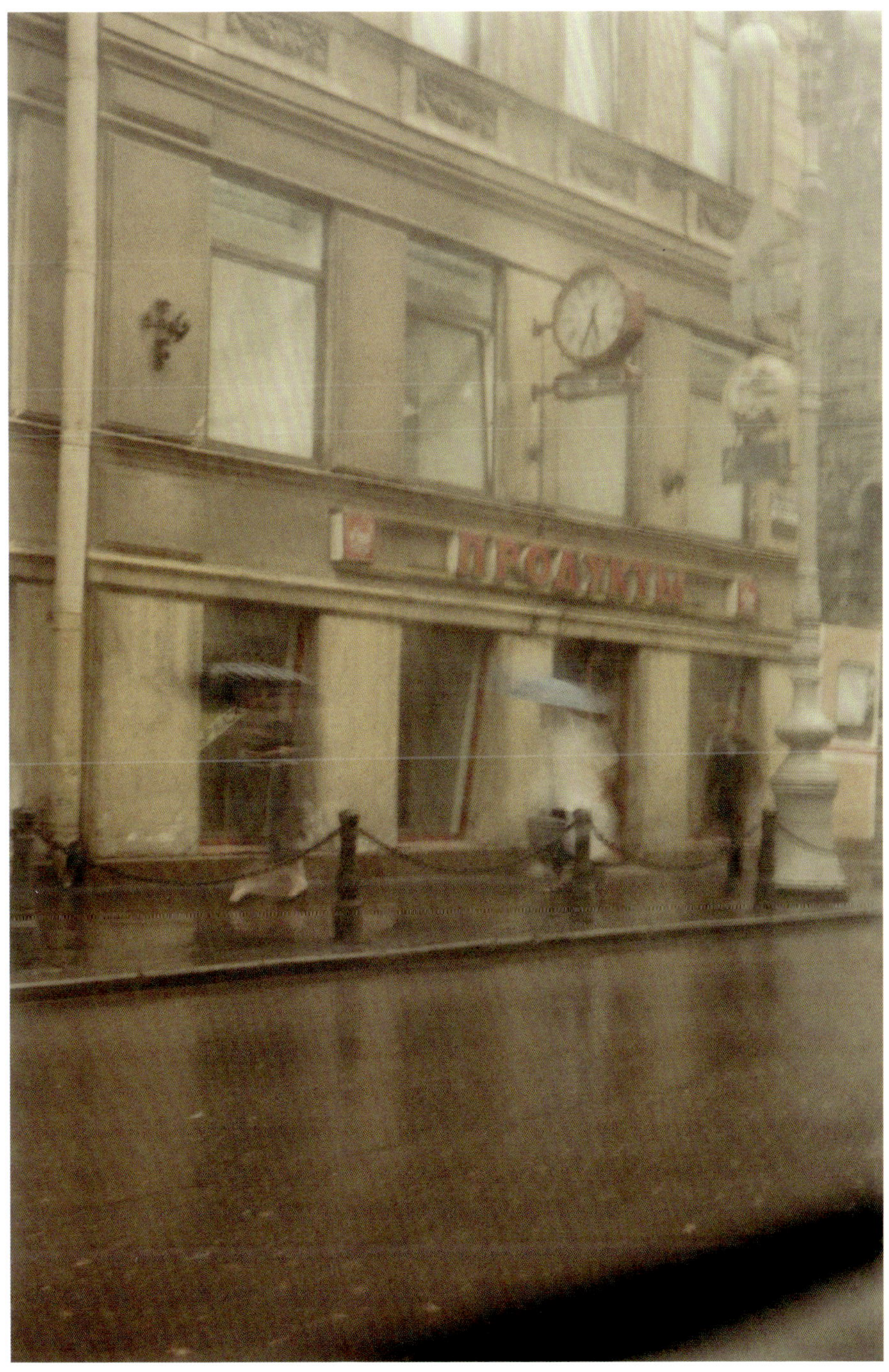

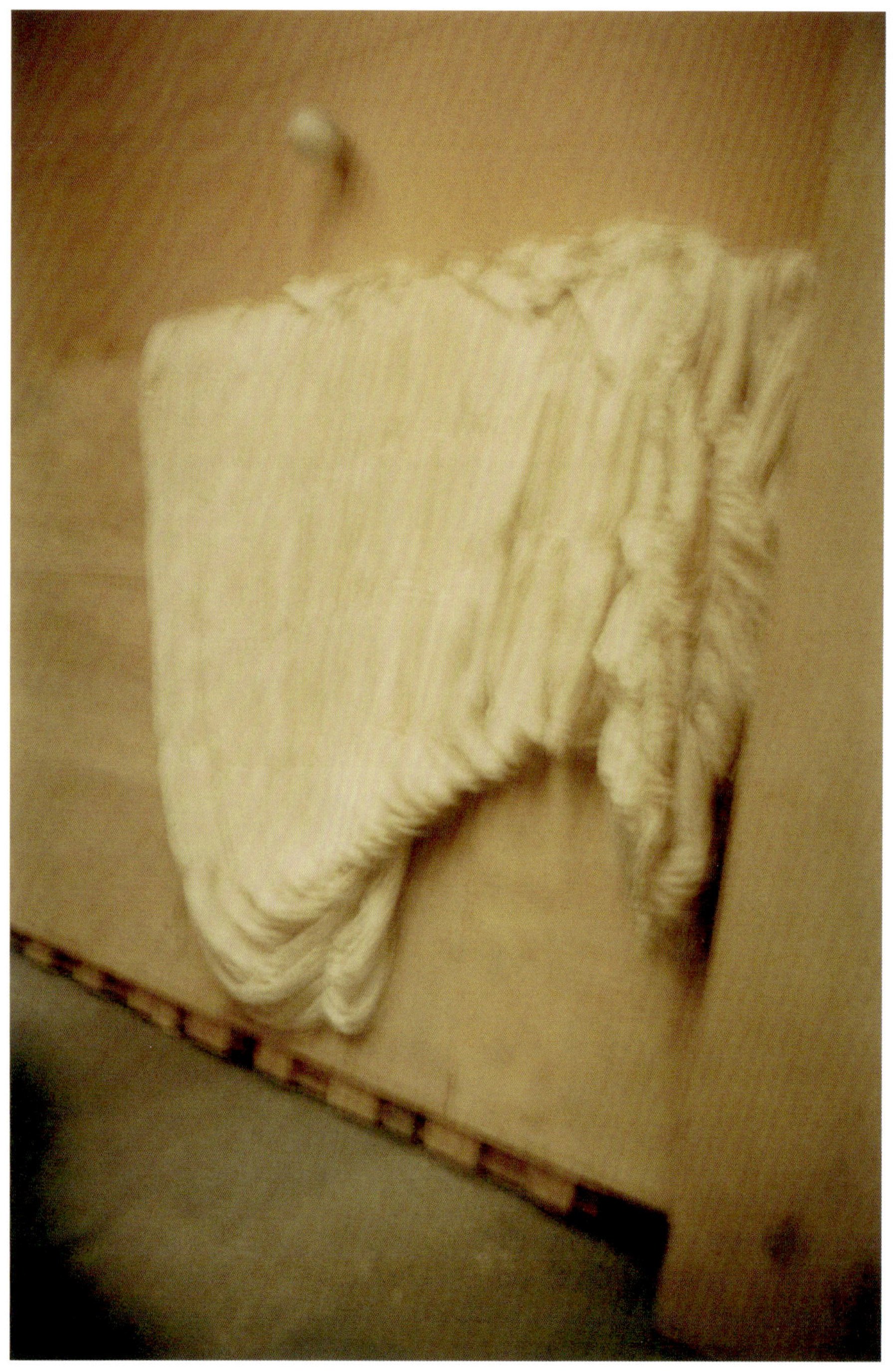

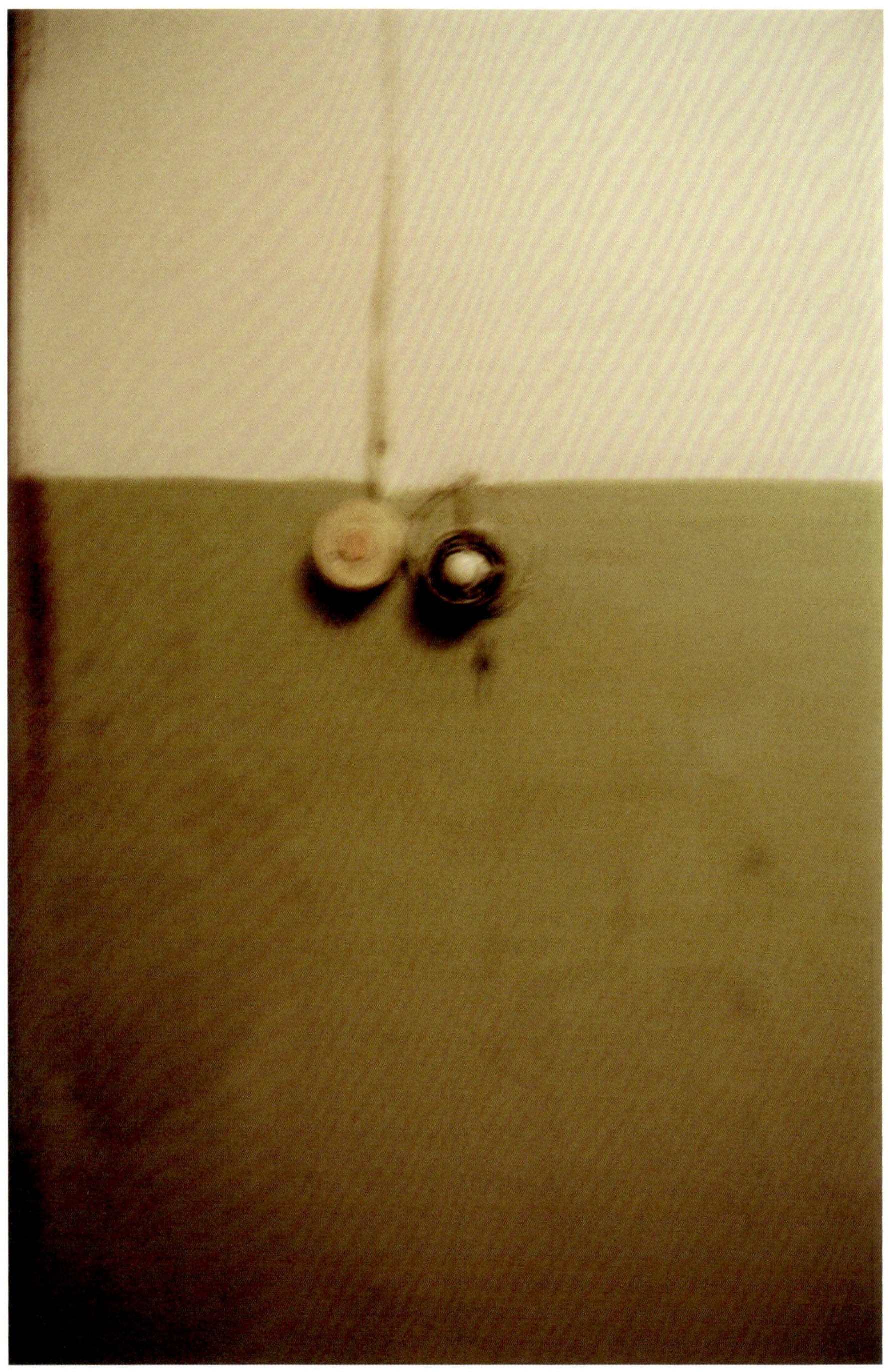

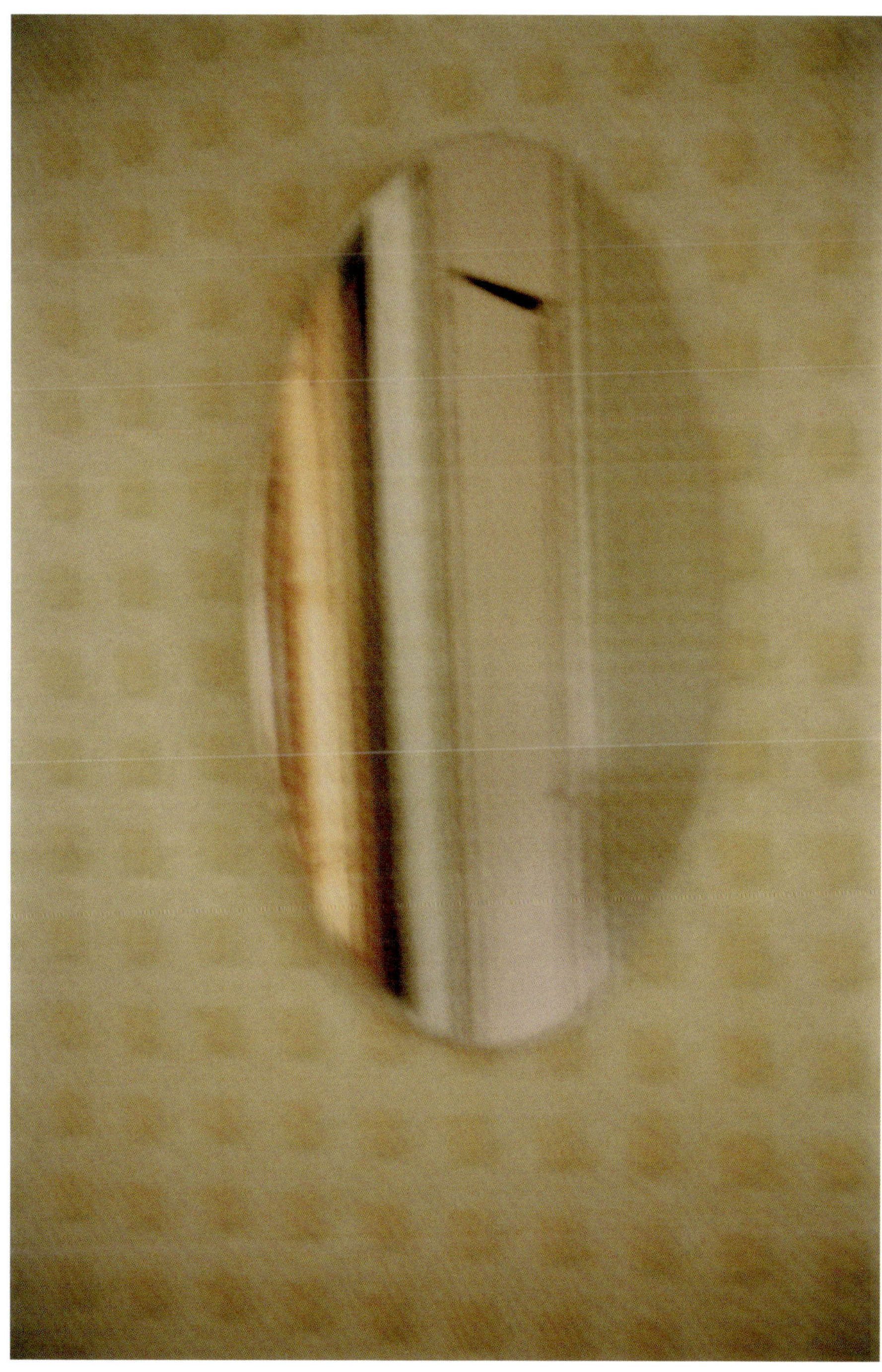

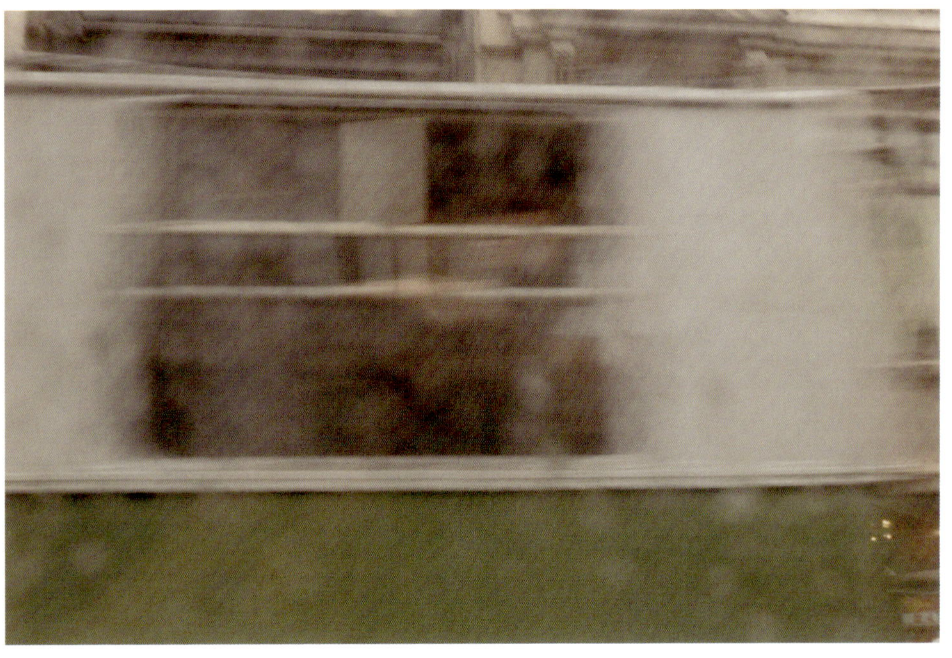

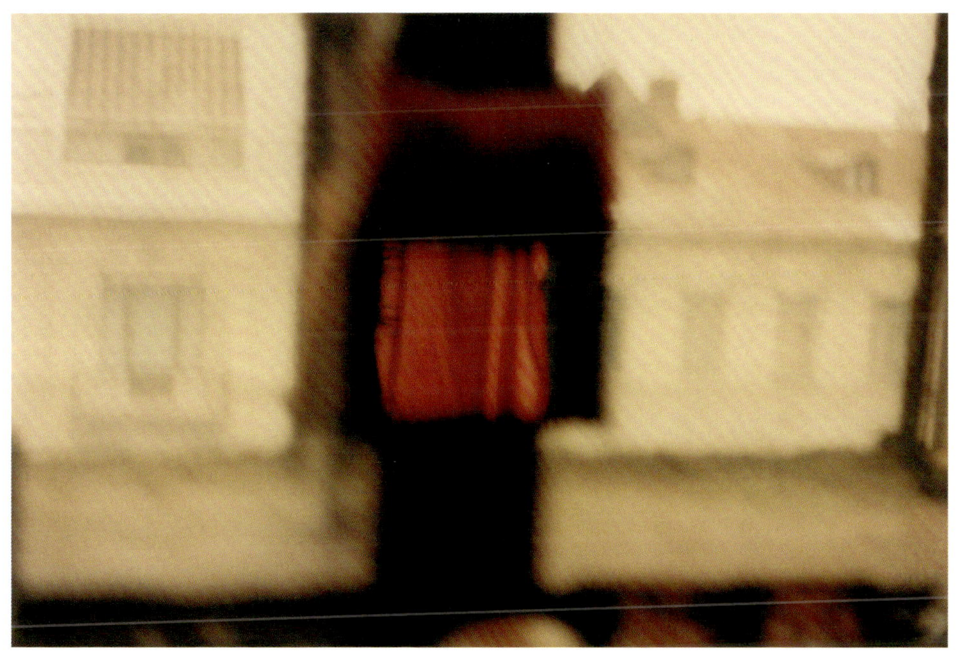

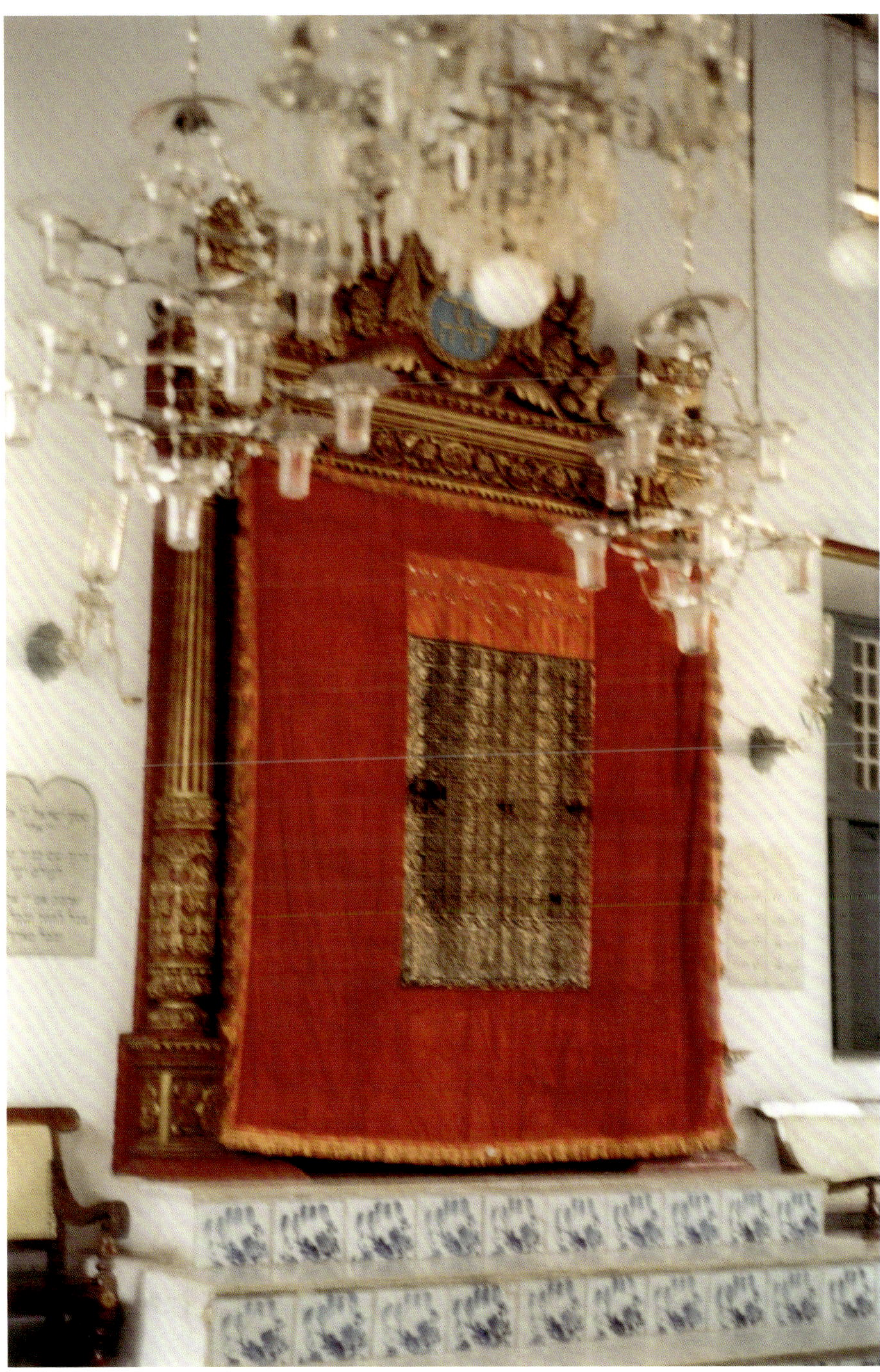

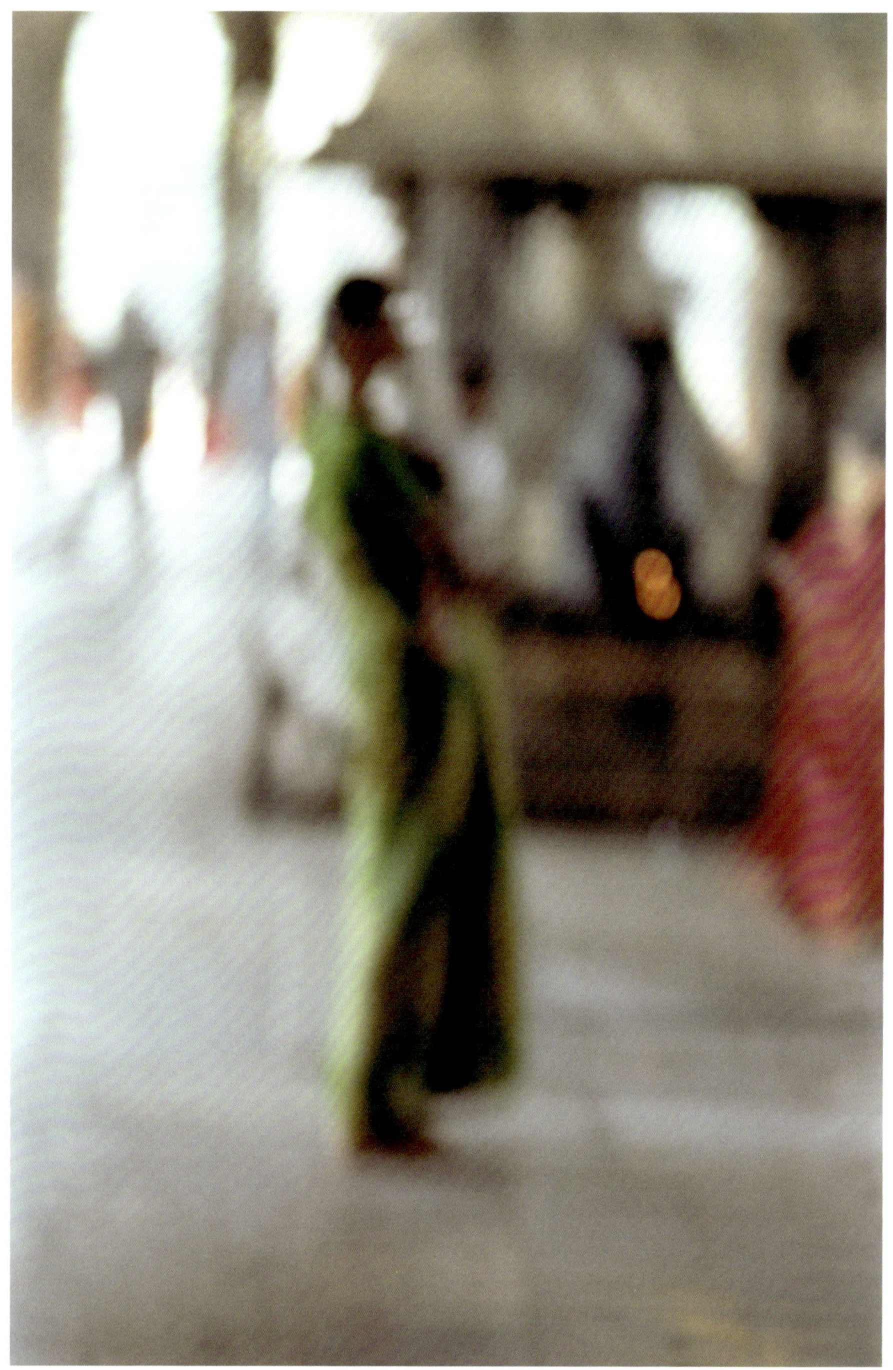

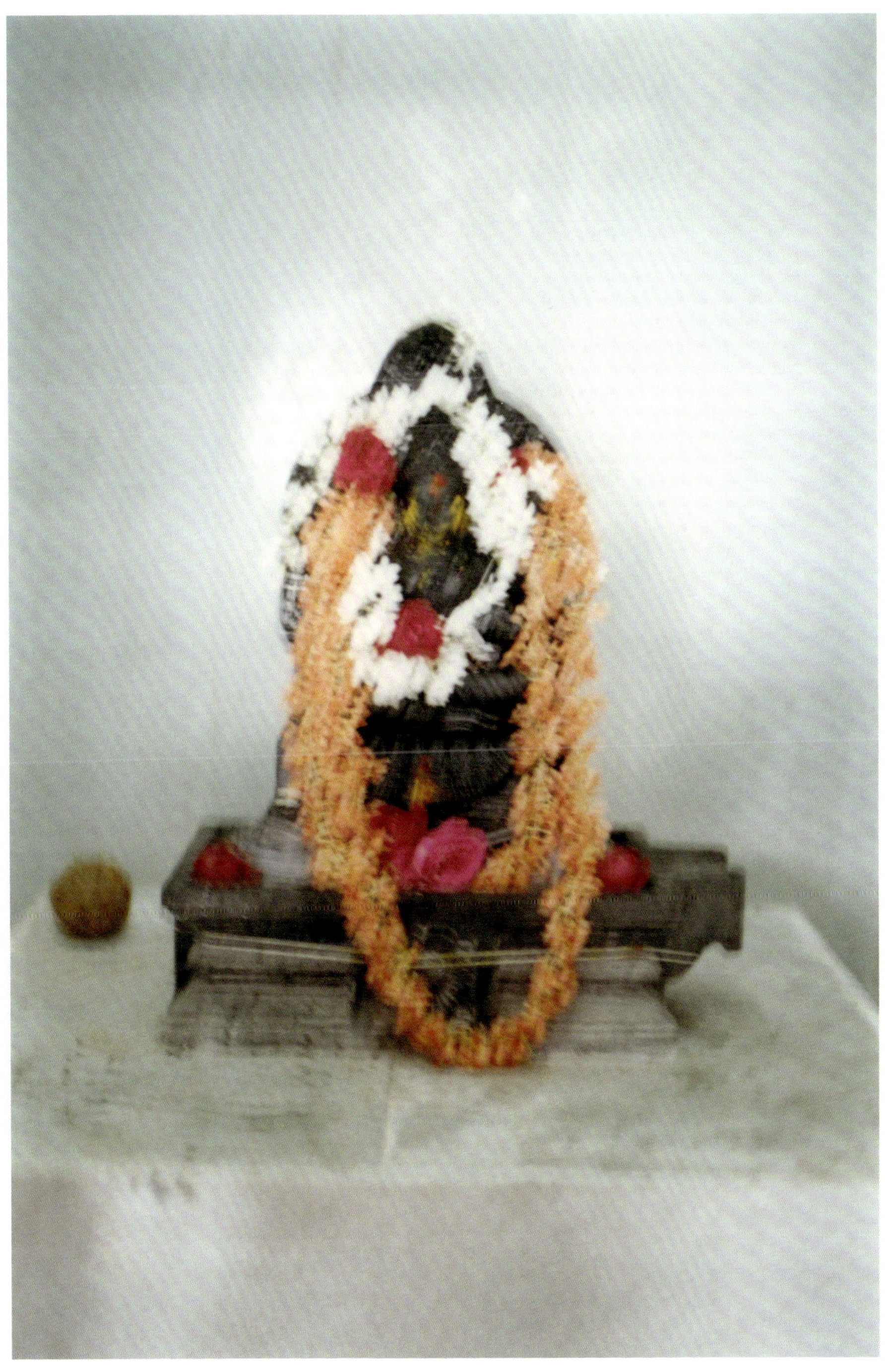

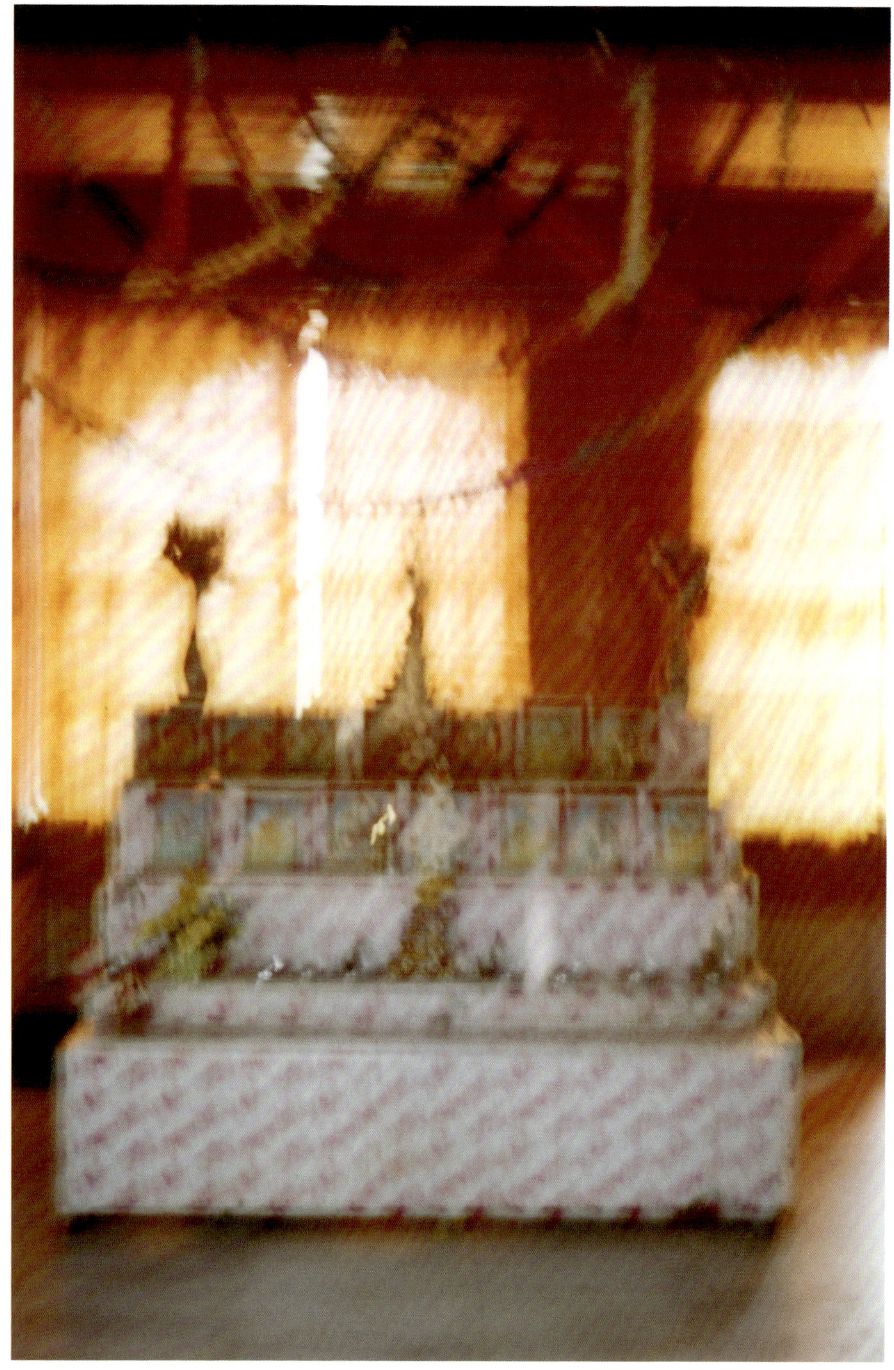

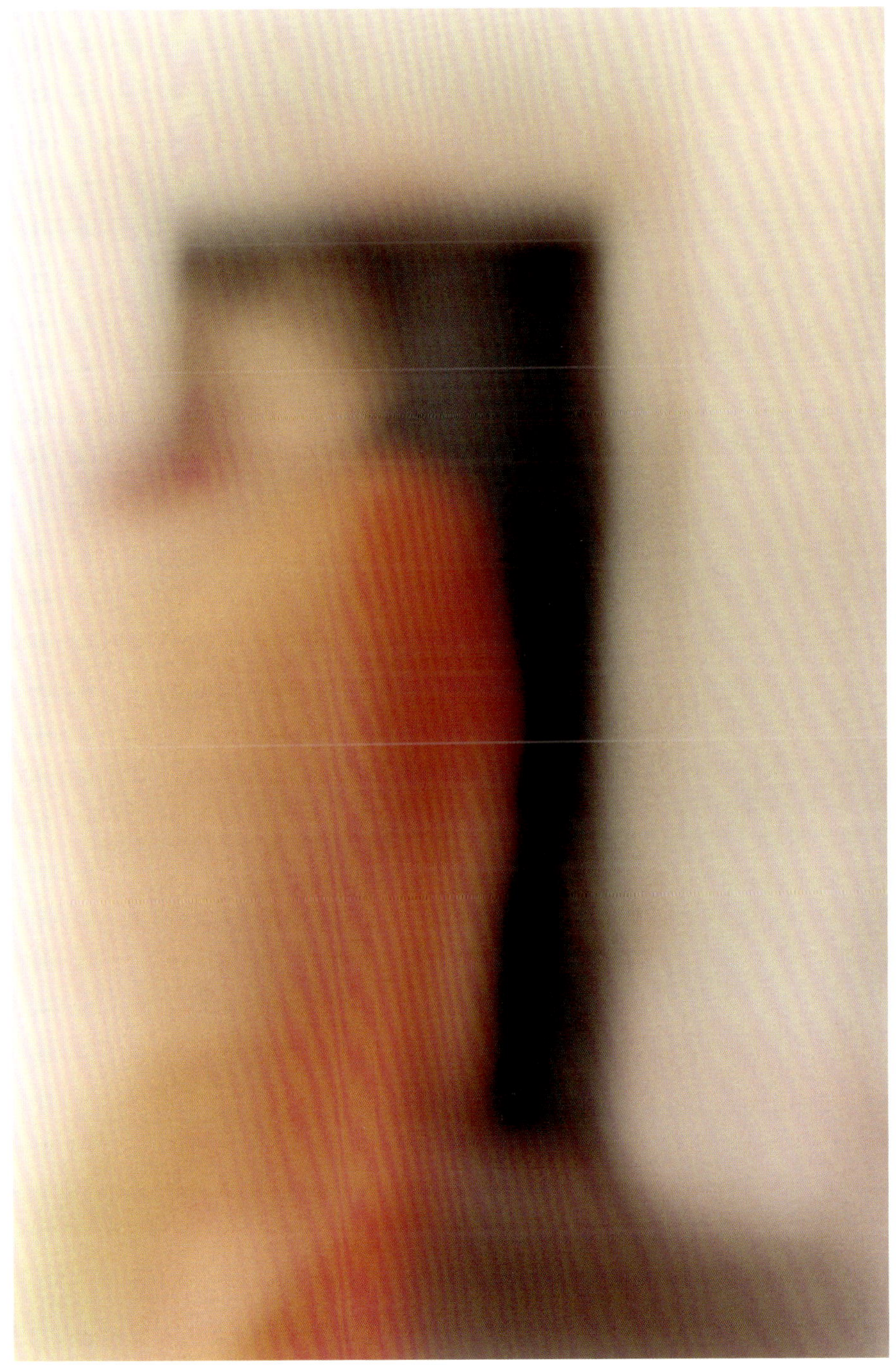

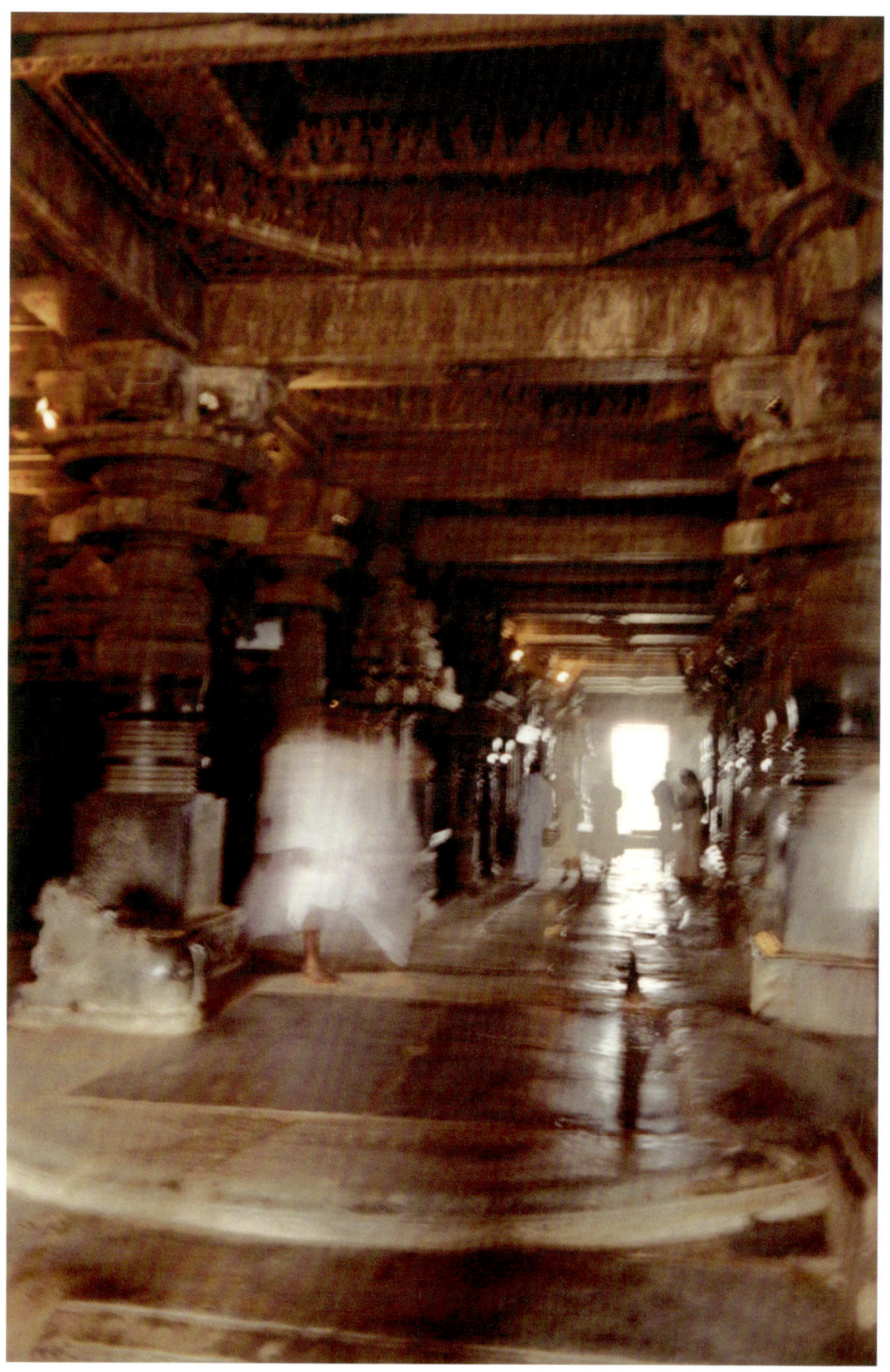

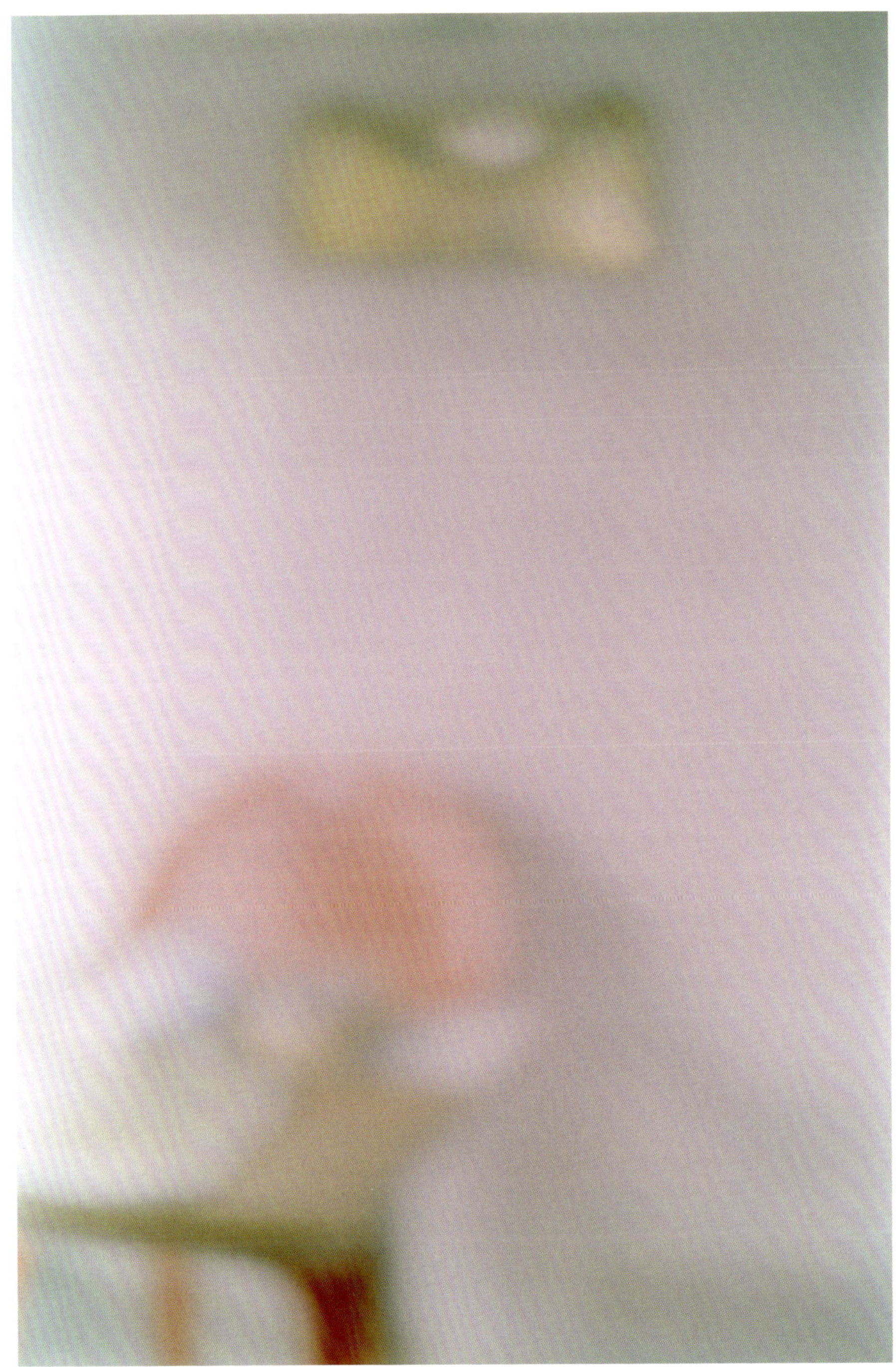

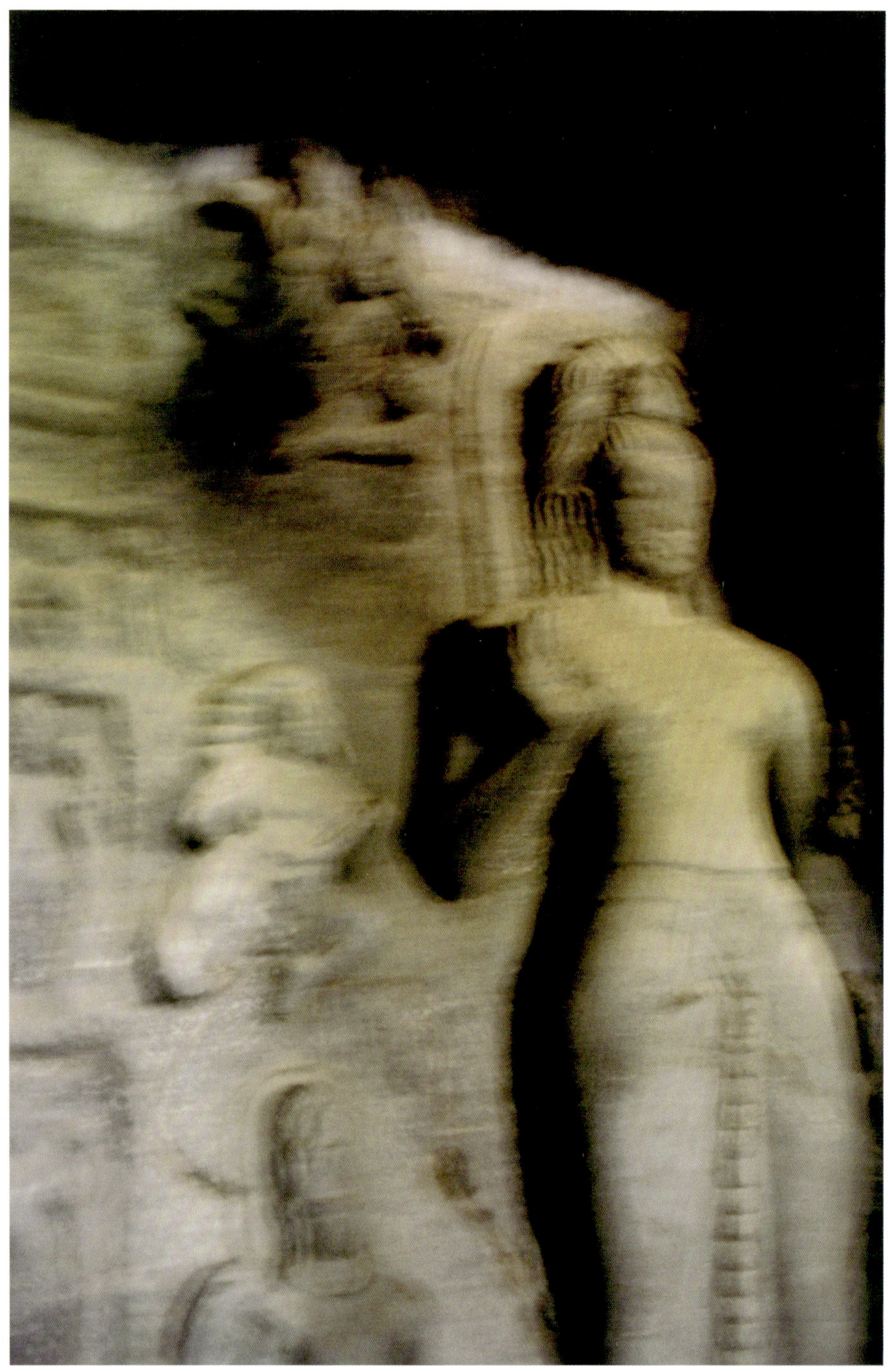

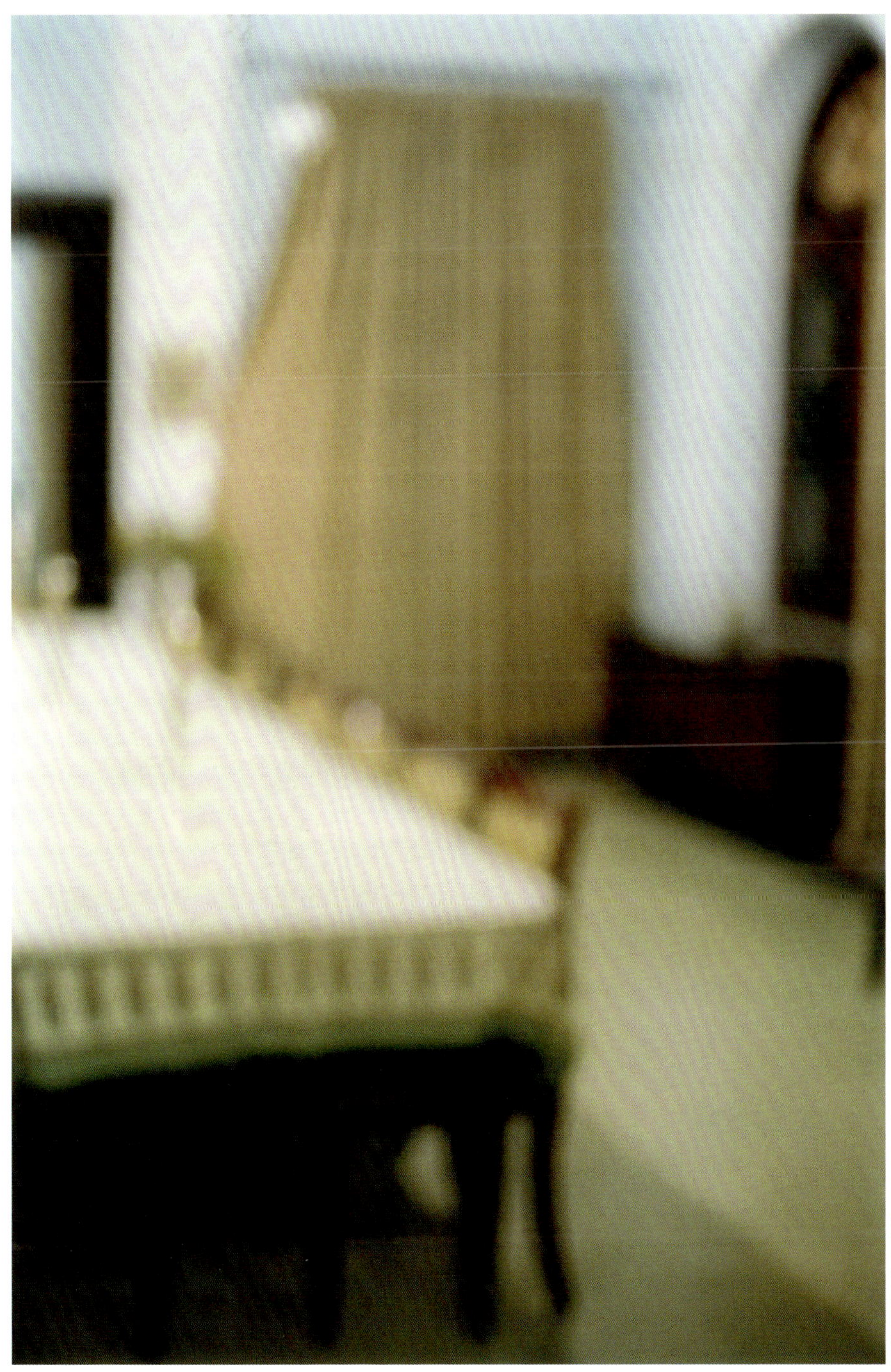

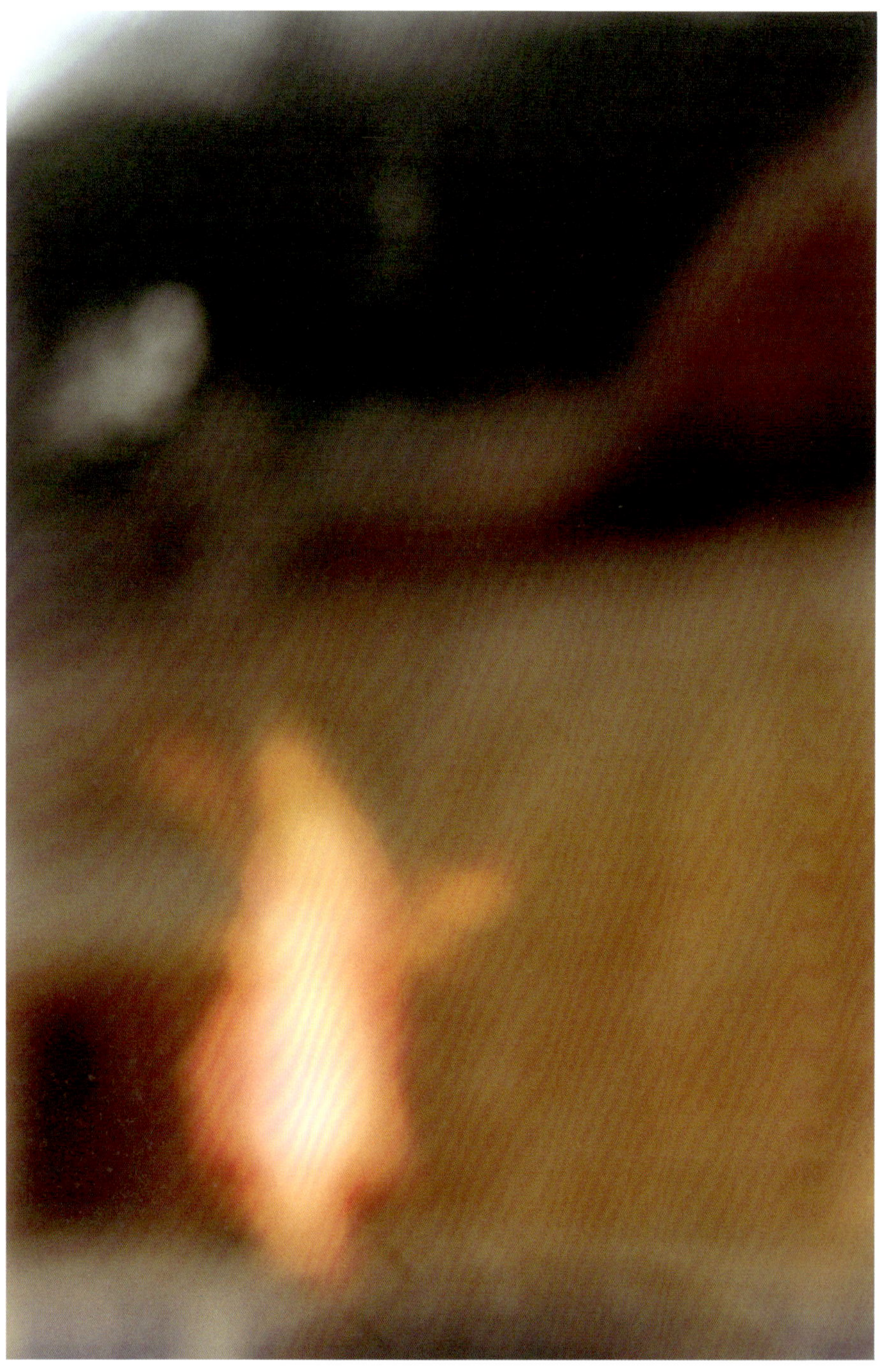

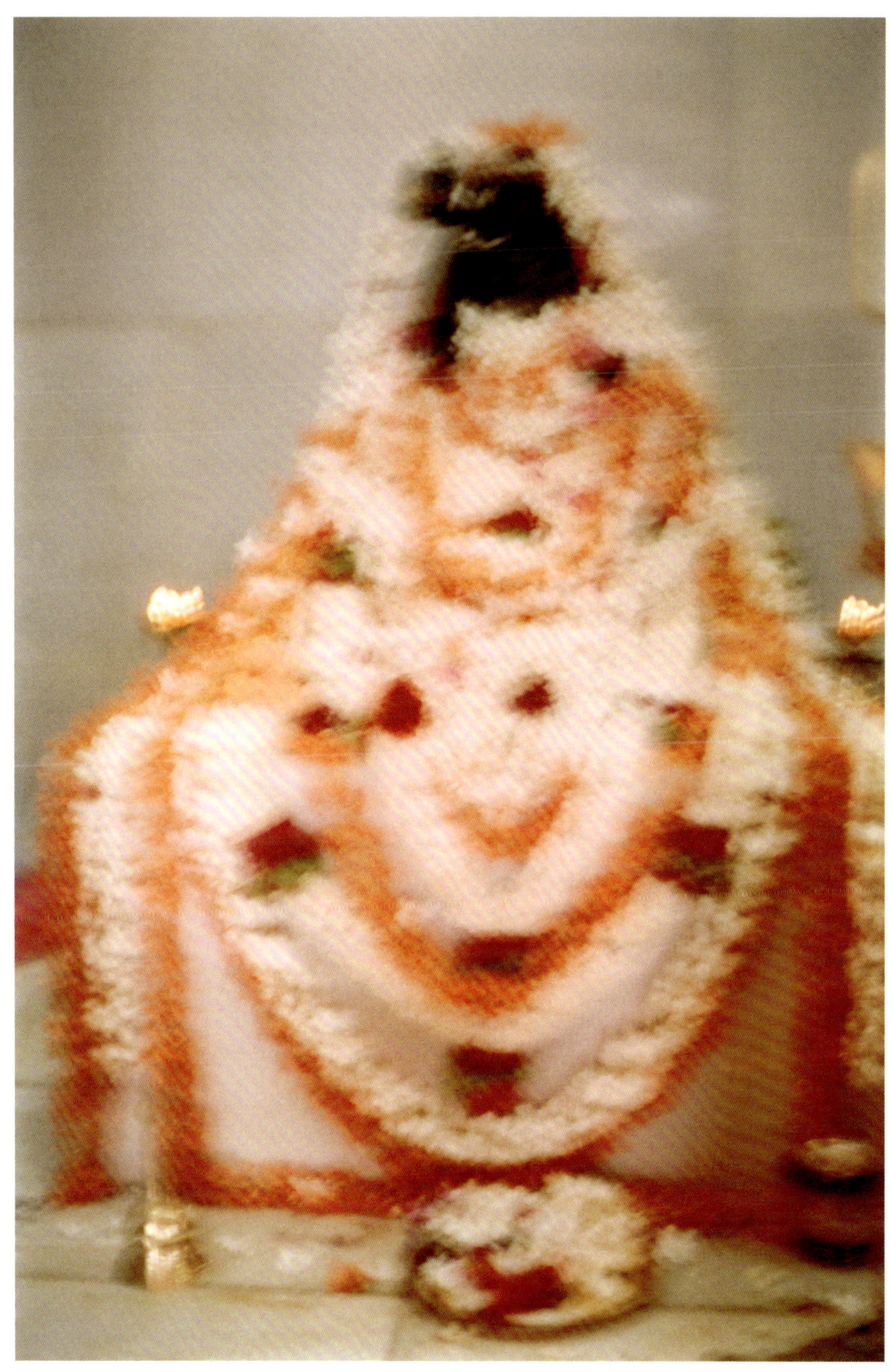

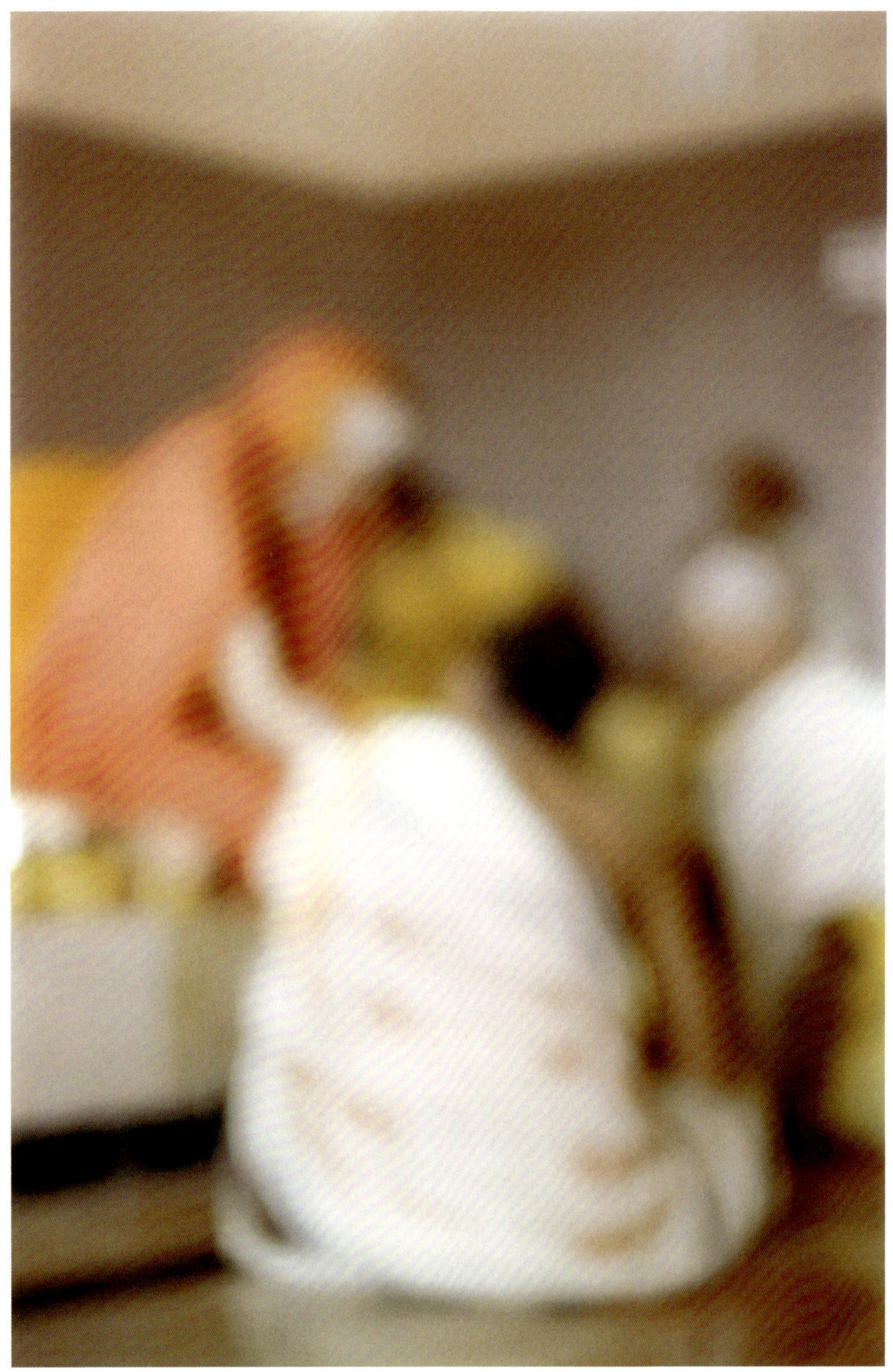

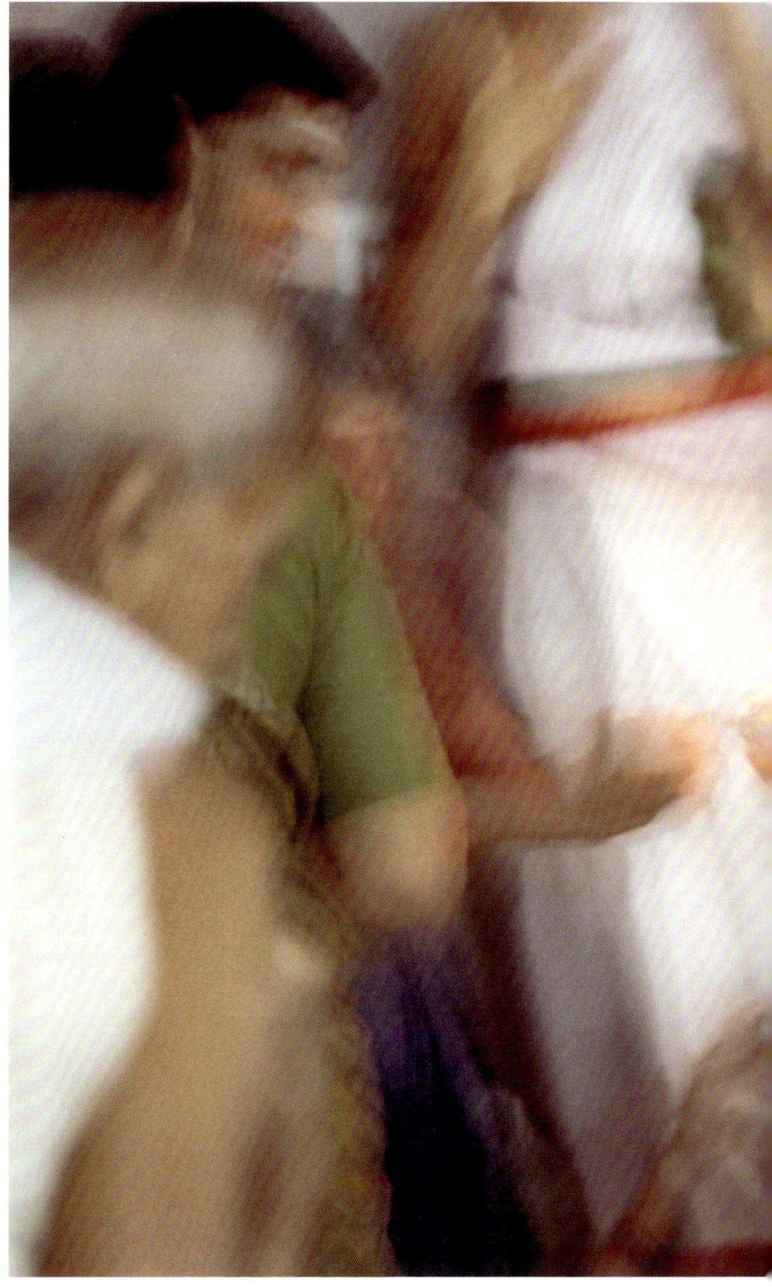

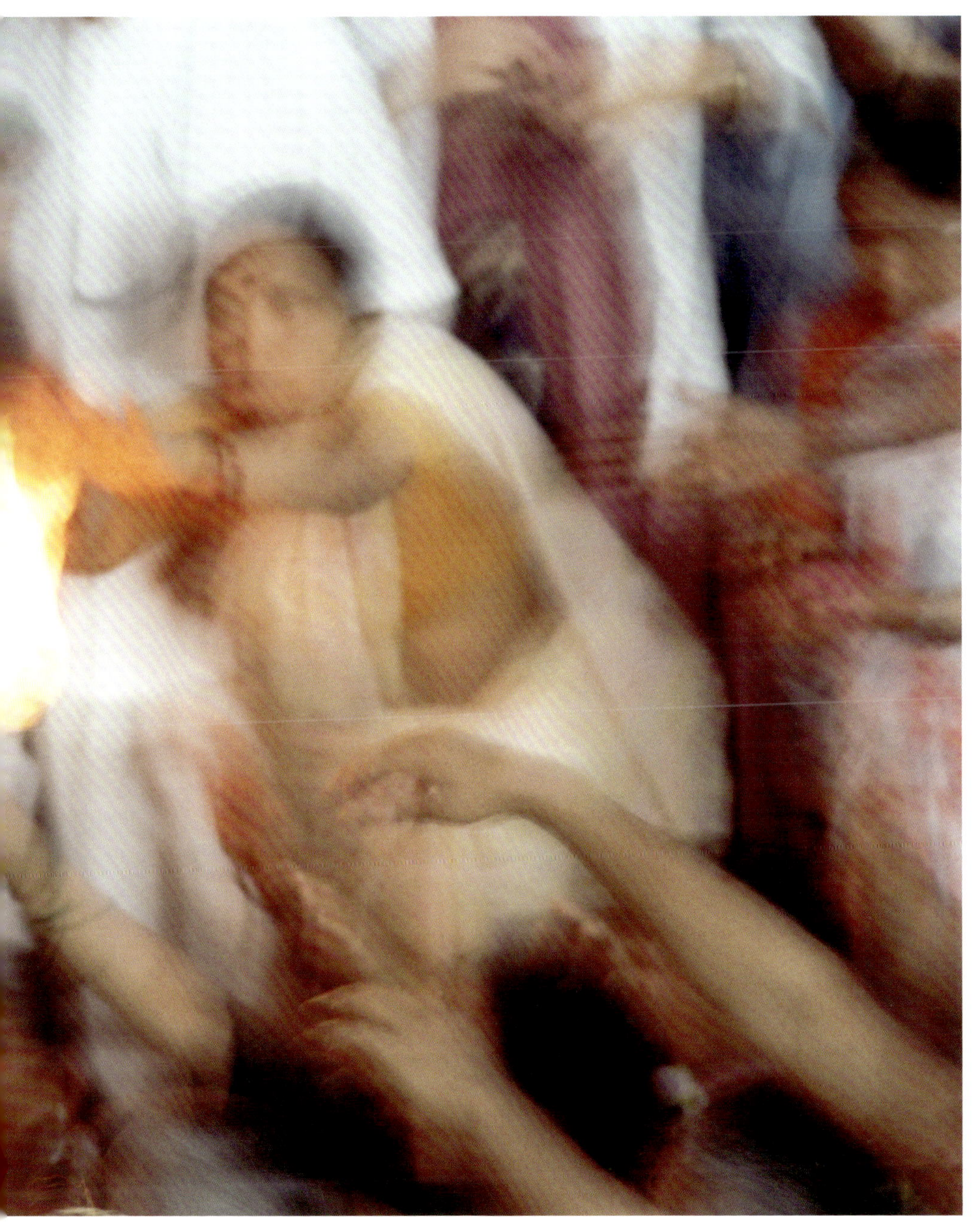

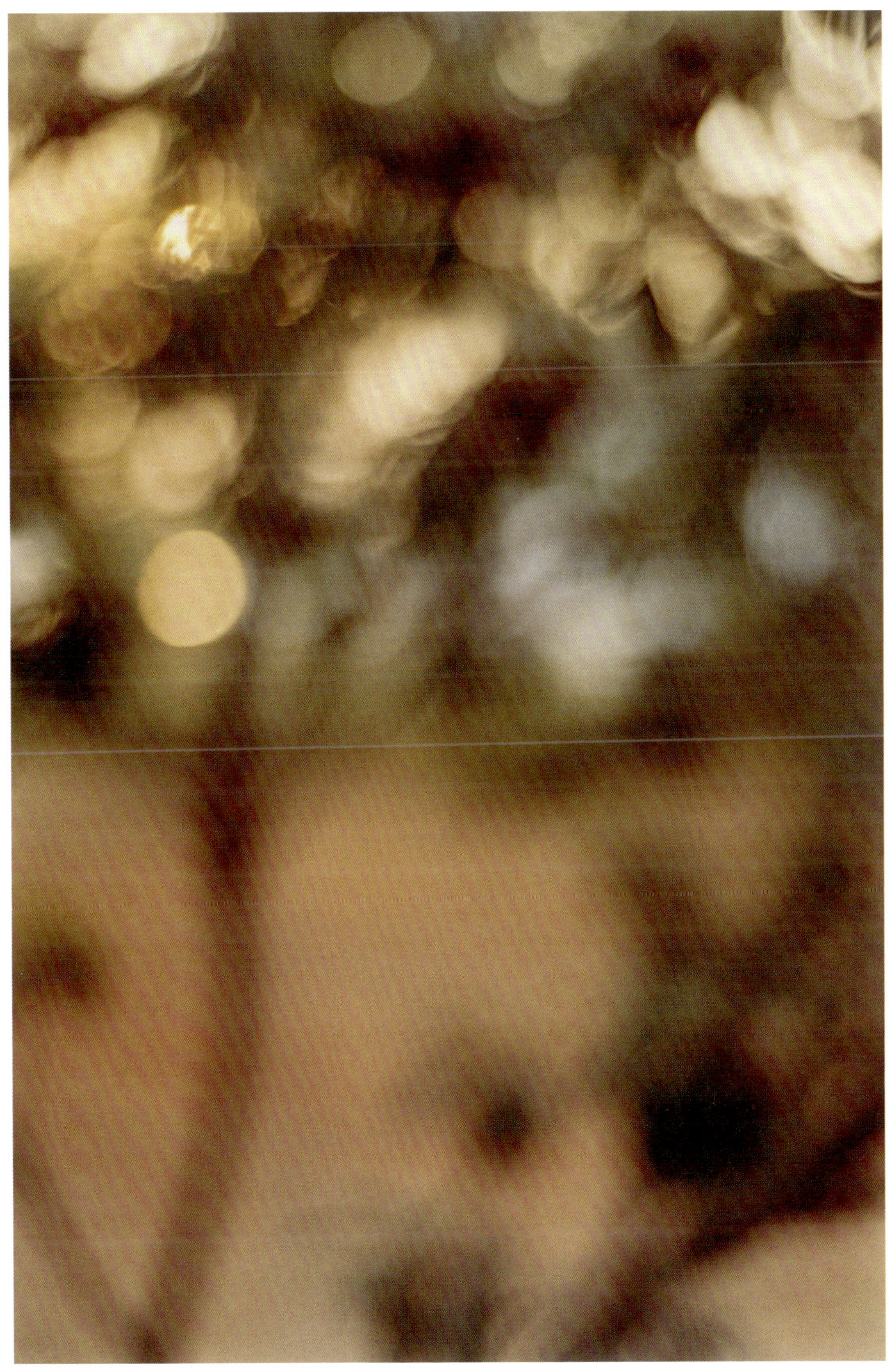

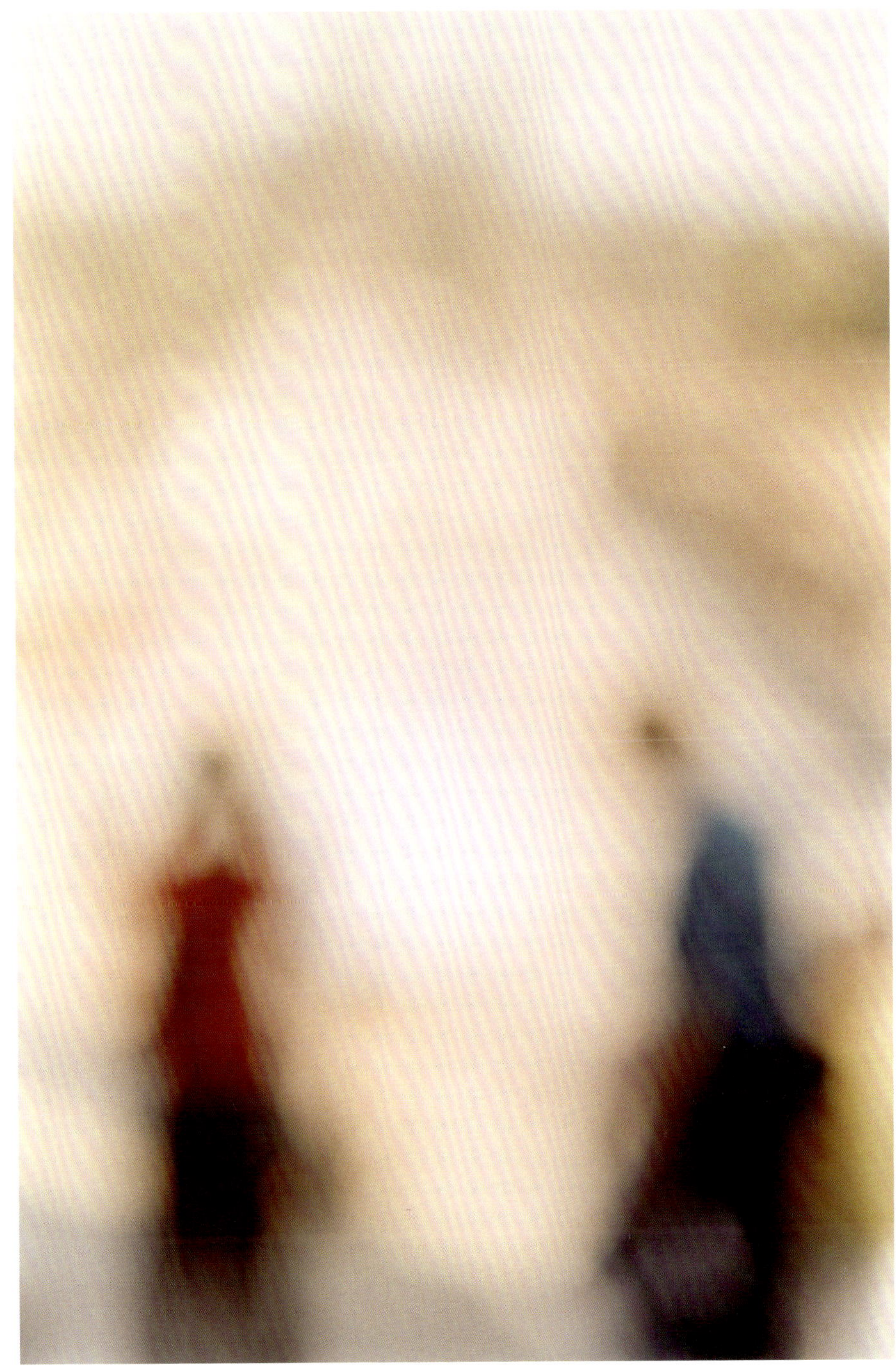

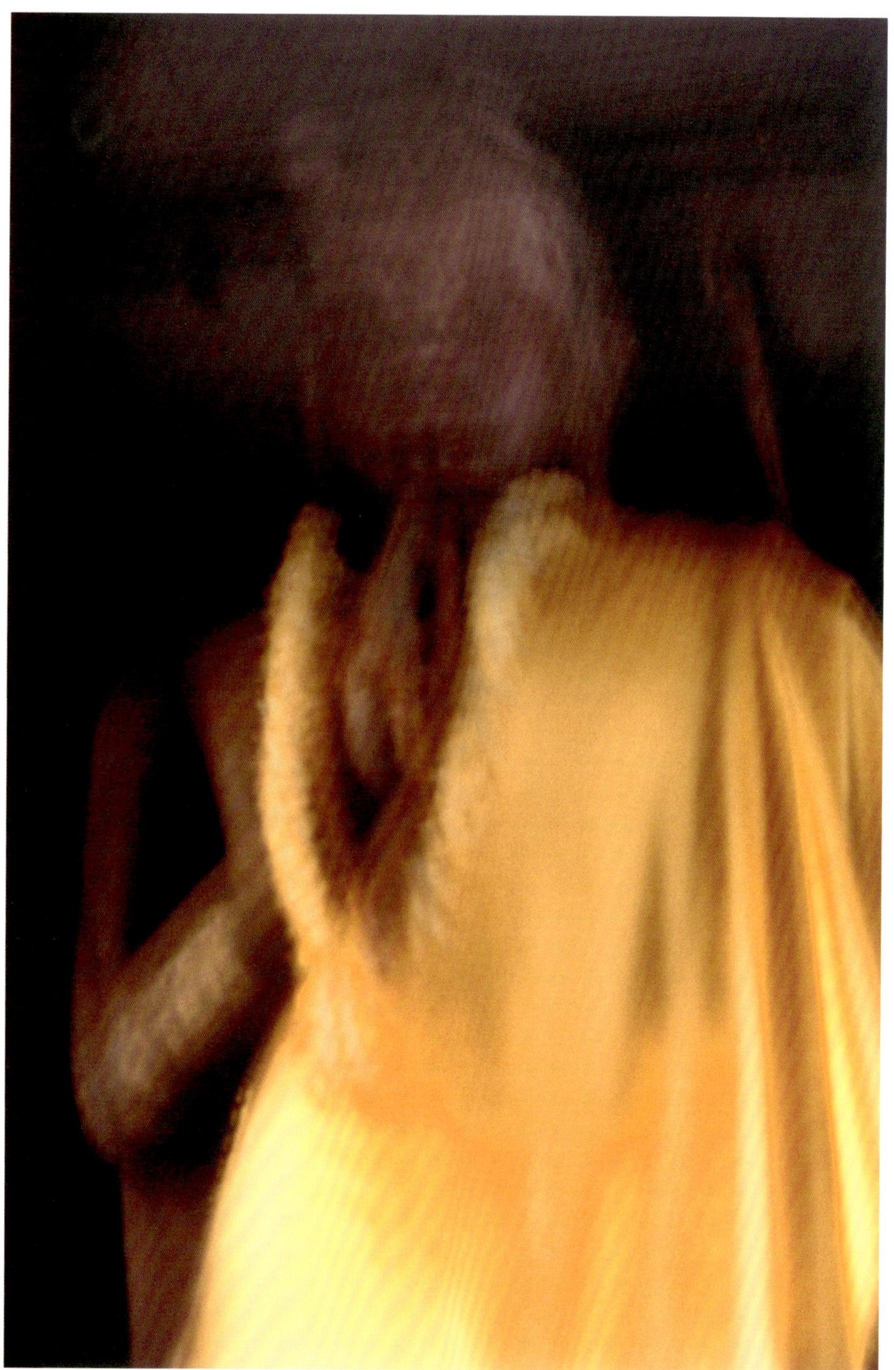

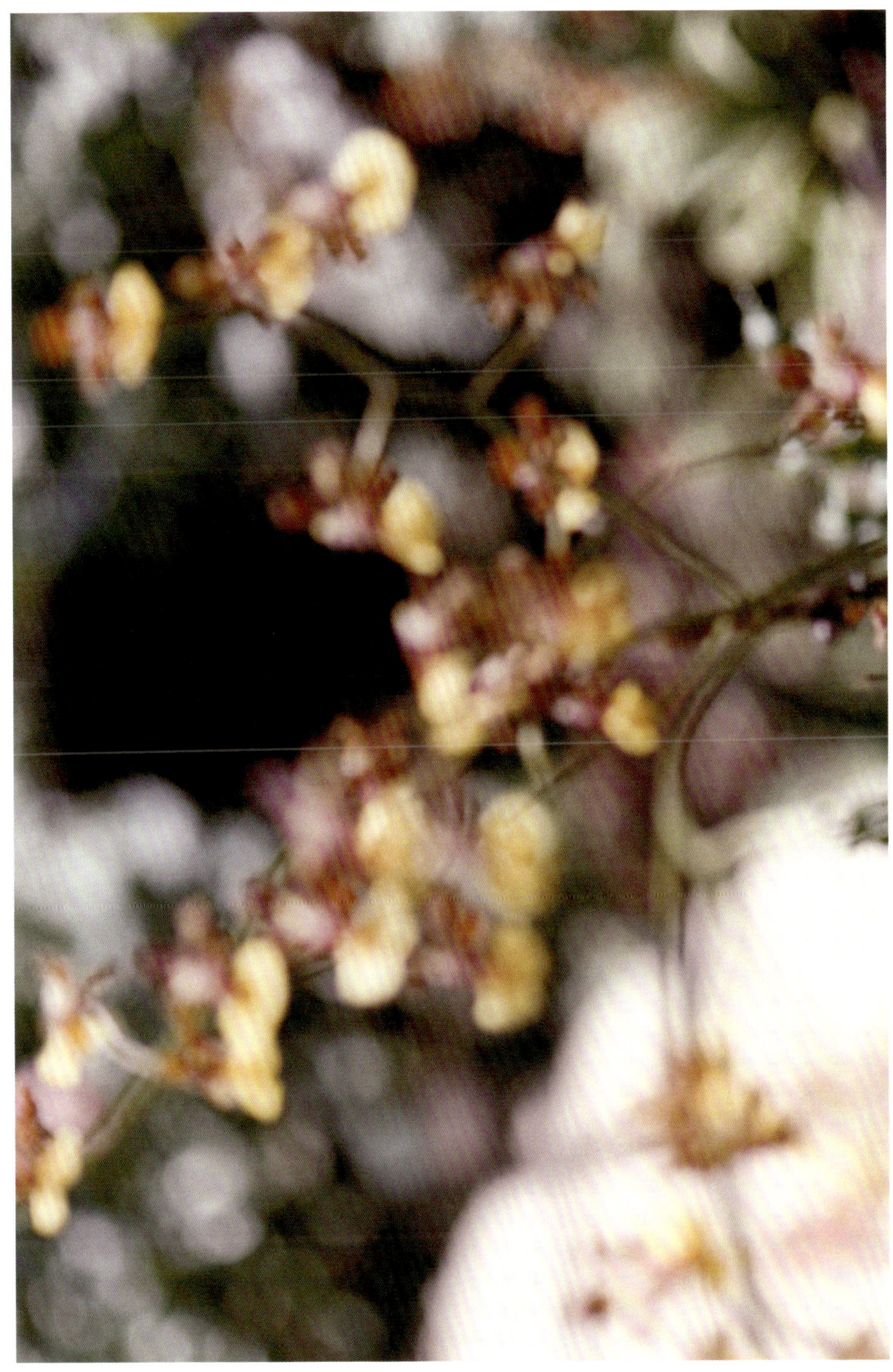

Captions

Acknowledgments

For making this project possible in many ways I wish to thank

Sri K. Pattabhi Jois, Herbert Henryson, Dylan & Géraldine Henryson, Stefan & Karis Henryson-Gibbs, Hérve & Baty Devaux, Mario Kramer, Thomas Trinter, Jon & Annie Abbott, Eddie Stern, Deborah G. Seidman, Linda Marrow, Johanna Davis, Jane Lombard, Ann McCoy, Skuta Helverson, Rosina Lardieri & Scott Spector, Monika Bravo, Chrysanne Stathacos, Shanti Thakur, David Perez, Sandra Olivo, Everyone at Kehrer

Concept Maxine Henryson
Photographs Maxine Henryson
Translation Marcella Sohme
English Editor Linda Marrow
Proofreading Katherine Stock-Ziegler
Book edit Mario Kramer & Maxine Henryson
Book design Deborah G. Seidman, New York &
Kehrer Design Heidelberg
Scans/prepress Intellifoto, New York
Printing and production Kehrer Design Heidelberg

Printed in Germany

Cover image Pâtisserie Boitsfort, Belgium 2003

Bibliographic information published
by the Deutsche Nationalbibliothek
The Deutsche Nationalbibliothek lists this
publication in the Deutsche Nationalbibliografie;
detailed bibliographic data are available
in the Internet at http://dnb.d-nb.de.

ISBN 978-3-939 583-47-9
Kehrer Verlag Heidelberg
www.artbooksheidelberg.com
www.maxinehenryson.com